The A&R Man

by

William "Mickey" Stevenson

Transcribed by Ashley Stevenson

from the Original Handwritten Manuscripts of

William "Mickey" Stevenson

Edited by

Sylvia V. Hillman

Front and Back Cover Photography: Novel Stevenson

Front/Back Cover Design: Angie Romasanta & Derek P. Larremore

ISBN: 069236634
ISBN-13: 978-0692366332

A Few Words From The Chairman...

"Mickey was a street cat, a wheeler-dealer, but I knew it was that same hustling quality that made him the superstar A&R man he was. He could match up any kind of team - writers, producers, artists - any combination..." "It was really with Mickey that I began something that was unique to my management style; building the structure around the person rather than fitting the person into the structure. People over structure would continue to dominate throughout the years..." "Right at the start, he went on the lookout for great musicians, combing even the seediest of bars and hangouts. If they could play, Mickey would bring 'em in, putting together the greatest house band that anyone could ever want. They called themselves The Funk Brothers..." "I (will) always remember Mickey Stevenson for his loyalty and dedication. He was one of the greatest creative forces during our formative years. He himself many times came up with a key idea, word or phrase on somebody else's production that helped make it a smash. A motivator, Mickey inspired greatness. He was tough but took care of his people. They loved him and so did I". (*Quotes sited with expressed permission from* **Berry Gordy's autobiography**, *"To Be Loved" 1994, 2013*)

"Mickey Stevenson is my brother, brother. He has not received his props. He was our first A&R man at Motown. Marvin wanted to be a crooner. Mickey was the one who turned Marvin around to become what we know and love! He convinced Marvin Gaye to sing rhythm and blues". (*Quote from Legendary songwriter and performer,* **Smokey Robinson** *via the 2010 presentation of the Lifetime Achievement Award to Mickey Stevenson at the California African American Museum.*)

"Mickey Stevenson was one of the first producers I met at Motown" (*Quote from* **Stevie Wonder**, *Motown Artist for Life, via the Hollywood Walk of Fame ceremonies for the Funk Brothers. March 2013*)

"When new musicians came into Motown and wanted to know, who's the power? It was Mickey". (*Quote from* **Jack Ashford**, *Funk Brothers percussionist via the documentary taping of "William Mickey Stevenson: Motown's First A&R Man"*)

CONTENTS

ACKNOWLEDGMENTS

When I was asked to write the acknowledgment section I paused; with all the people I've encountered in my life, where do I start? I've had the pleasure over the years to meet a ton of people and had the opportunity to learn from most of them and the pleasure to teach others, thank God. The acknowledgement page is where everyone searches franticly to see if they were mentioned before they even read the book. Well I'm one step ahead of you. Go ahead and insert your name here, right there in that blank space under the arrow.   ↓

First I want to especially thank you, _____ for picking up this book, for reading a little bit and for marking your name in it, cause now you gotta buy it!

Now just so we're clear, these thank you's and acknowledgments have been compiled over 50 plus years in the entertainment industry where I've met more personalities than I have met people LOL! Yet every encounter has led me one more step forward, creatively and has inspired me more than you know. So once again thank you _____. And just to prove to the world that these acknowledgments are in no specific order, I put you first but we both know God comes first and we all follow after him.

I'm so thankful for the time spent with my talented mother, Kitty Stevenson, my brother Martin, and my sister Elaine. I'm grateful for the family that stands by me today; Lonnie, my brother. My sons; Craig, Mickey Jr., Darrell, Damian, Novel, Brian, Patrick Benoit, Justin Holley. To my daughters, who stand by me with unwavering love and devotion; Ashley, Mikkia, Amber and Taylor. My nieces, nephews and grands; Junebug, Dena, LaRetha-Lynn, Seer, William R the 5th , Rachel, Novel Amir, Mya, Cincere, Promise, Chozen, Prince, Melisa, Monet, and Jerome. I'm so blessed to have you in my life. To my friends; a special thanks to Berry Gordy; I got this chief, to Ruth Robinson; aint it nice to leave all the B.S. alone ha ha! To my friend John Payne; a volcano in shorts, Pat Gills, Paul Riser; who blew his way out of the pit. David Whitfield, Ka-Ron Lehman, Johnny Nash; oh God still has the face of a 16 yr old kid! Ron Hasley, Mel Carter, Roland Bynum; bind 'em Roland and don't let em get away. Mickey Gentile, Mary Card, Kem Anyanwu, to Larkin Arnold; who had the heart to go after Marvin Gaye. Marva Farmer, Robert Thompson-So, I'm still waiting on my cut! Xavier Gardner, Russ Regan, The Glassman's; well you can find them taking over Florida. Jennifer Holiday; you're my Dream Girl and that's the gospel truth! Norman Tillman, Sidney Miller, Lowell; what a fan, Reza, Duke Faker; thank you Duke, you're always at the top of your game! Greg Middleton, the beautiful Kristin Volk, to Peter Andrews; "I said put that glass away!" Jack Ashford; The Chunk of Funk. My brother, Norm Nixon; the traveling man. Emit Cash, Lewis Khoury; welcome back my brother. Jennie Bell; there's no denying you. Erroll Jackson, Duane Moody, Ashley Culp, Cornelius Grant, Pedro Ferre; who will soon be the president of Mexico, Ole'! My friend Jeffery Allen, to Jane Dashow; the world has yet to see the talent you hold. Ken Dashow; we shall find a way to let the world have a peek. Jeff Elmassian, Mary Catherine Finney, Glynn Turman, Leon Levy, Woody King, My jive ass friend Patricia Hodges of Hodges, James, and Smith...

Janie Bradford; you're always walking with joy. Susan Weaving; let's do this one! Henrik Henriksen, David Fisher, Ron Lamont, Ray Parker Jr., Rickey Williams, Cupid my angel, Blinky Williams, to Jeffery Osborn, James Sanders; no one can copy your greatness. Virgil and Brenda Roberts. Louis Price, Robert Gordy, Berry Gordy the 4th aka B-4. Alex Marino, H.B. Barnum, Martha Reeves; aren't you glad you picked up my phone? Robert Montalvo; I see your vison. Joe Jimason; put some draws on them cards, Robin Williams; you're on your own but not alone sista-sista. Jim Jecknavorian; and then you got in your car and drove away LOL! Judge Strong, Aretha Franklin; we did it Aretha and we still doin' it! Max Julien; It's not a fantasy – Max is Back and That's a Fact! Valarie Benning; smile girl – I'm still here. To the Twins; Adele and Estelle – My Prayer Warriors! What a Blessing! Donald Douroux; take the phone out your pocket & turn it on! Nanni White Cross, Edna Anderson-Owens; "Berry for ever. Very clever", Bomba Lea; you're amazing just the way you are. Kim Weston, Melanie Burke, Sandra, Vanessa, Elaine and Betty-Ann. A special thanks to Sylvia V. Hillman for proofreading and editing this book. To Janks Morton Jr. and Derek P. Larremore for assisting with the publication of this book. To Novel my son for the wonderful photographs for the front and back cover of this book. To Ruth Robinson for her input, constructive criticism and love. To B'anca for insisting that I write the A&R Man. To my daughter Taylor, for being my daughter Taylor. And most of all to my daughter Ashley, for her tenacity, creative input and unselfish devotion.

AND A VERY SPECIAL Thanks to MY BROTHER AND LIFE LONG FRIEND THE INCREDIBLE Smokey Robinson, God has always been with you.

PROLOGUE

Some of the most important things I learned as an A&R man (A&R stands for Artists and Repertoire) that helped me throughout my career in the entertainment business are; 1) Ability; 2) Material; 3) Charisma; 4) Absolute Focus; and 5) A Relentless Pursuit to be The Best. Three of those five will make you a star. Four or more will make a Superstar!

Artists like Smokey Robinson, Stevie Wonder, Beyoncé, Eminem and Justin Timberlake; it doesn't matter who they are, or which road they traveled to the world of entertainment, if these essentials are there, they will be unstoppable!

With that being said and understood, I gotta tell you this - The A&R man was and is the backbone of the record business.

The world of entertainment is a game with a purpose. The game is to have fun and enjoy yourself while the purpose is to diligently pursue your dream.

The artists we signed to Motown were some of the finest in the world. The writers and producers were without a doubt some of the most gifted. Every book I've read on the subject, mentions the order and sequence in which the artists arrived at Motown, the hits they sang, the songs that were written, even their producers. These books were very well written, personally and historically, giving you a play by-play description of the Motown dynasty.

They were written by music historians and Motown artists like Diana Ross, who penned Secrets of a Sparrow, Gladys Knight's, Between Each Line of Pain and Glory, Raynoma Gordy Singleton's Berry, Me, and Motown, Otis Williams' Temptations, Mary Wilson's Dreamgirl and Supreme Faith: My Life as a Supreme as well as David Ritz's Divided Soul, the biography depicting the life of Marvin Gaye, Smokey Robinson's Smokey: Inside My Life, and academic Gerald Early's One Nation Under a Groove: Motown and American Culture. Even writer Gerald Posner's Motown: Music, Money, Sex and Power had some merit.

Berry Gordy, the chairman himself, got into the act with To Be Loved: The Music, the Magic, the Memories of Motown. His book not only gives you the chronological order of the artists and their hits, it also comes with his personal collection of historical photographs. He didn't miss a beat. By the way, neither did Diana when she came back with her latest book, a biography by J. Randy Taraborrelli, simply titled Diana Ross: A Biography.

I won't bore you by retelling the same stories written in all the other books. What I am gonna tell you about is the other side; the side that only a few of us were privileged to know about, experience or even dared talk about. Since I was in the mix up to my neck, I can tell you the way it was and the way it happened to me. Through my eyes, I'm going to reveal the inner workings that helped keep "the Motown machine" rolling day and night. You will get to know some of the people responsible for the Motown success; folks like me and other unsung heroes.

Every book ever written about Motown speaks of William "Mickey" Stevenson, The A&R Man who carried a big stick and knew how to use it. But never really touched on who I was, what I did and how I did it. More importantly, why did the man we called The Chairman, Berry Gordy; make Mickey Stevenson the backbone of Motown? Why did BG grant me that kind of power over all those musicians, writers, producers, and most of the artists?

The only way to answer those questions and explain my contribution to the Motown phenomenon is to let you know from my personal point of view as an A&R Man as well as my own personal journey to becoming one of many who helped build the Motown dynasty. Yes, as the first A&R Man for Motown - I set the standard!

The music of Motown was a gift from God to the world at a time when the world needed it most. I thank God I was allowed to be a part of that gift.

JULY 14, 2003

On July 14, 2003, I was on the golf course with Smokey Robinson, Robert Gordy, Harvey Fuqua, and B.IV, (B-4) the nickname we used for Berry Gordy's son.

We were on the ninth hole and B.IV was kicking our butts. I remember it was the ninth because I needed that hole to break even. Right in the middle of my back swing, Smokey's cell phone started ringing on the highest volume - blasting over the entire course. He answered the phone talking just as loud as he always does.

We're used to his phone ringing all the time, so I just stopped and waited for him to either get off the bloody phone or to carry his butt somewhere else to hold his conversation. He never turns that damn phone off. And on that day, it really pissed me off, because I was losing. I don't like to lose, ever. Fortunately for him this particular call was from The Chairman himself, Mr. Berry Gordy, Jr. Smokey, answered the usual questions - who was there and who was winning. Then he handed me the phone...

"Hey Mickey, I heard you're playing well. I'll come right over. How many strokes are you going to give me?" he asked.

"Strokes? Give you strokes! Are you kidding? First of all, giving you strokes would be like fighting a wounded lion. Second, with his thirty years of youth, B.IV is already kicking everybody's ass, so I don't need to be bothered with a young tiger and an old lion."

As Berry laughed, "B.IV is pretty good, huh?" you could hear the pride in his voice.

"Mick, what I called to tell you is; I need you, Smokey and Robert at the TV interview for the Motown museum we're building in Detroit.

"It's going to be an incredible museum. Not only will it be about the artists, but the writers, the producers, and all the people that helped make the music of Motown, music that the world came to love."

He didn't just say he wanted me there...

"Mick, I need you. You were one of the guys that helped make it all happen, along with the producers, the writers, the musicians, everybody. Being the first A&R man of Motown made you a very important part of the company. So I need you there at the interview. Mickey, you are definitely one of Motown's unsung heroes."

Hearing those words gave me such a lump in my throat I couldn't speak for a moment.

"Are you all right?" his voice asked through the phone as I pulled myself together.

"Yeah, Chief, I'm fine! Just tell me when and where."

I knew he could hear the emotion in my voice. It was hard for me to hide it. He said Edna, from his office, would call me in the morning with the details.

"No problem, Chief."

I handed Smokey's phone back to him, "Are you all right, brother man?"

"I'm fine, my brother, just fine."

A wonderful feeling came over me. The significance of belonging again; a sense of pride and love that I can't explain except to say it washed over me. The kind of feeling I had at Motown over fifty years ago. I never thought I would have those feelings again, but here they were. Oh my God, with my emotions running wild, my mind started racing back in time over the years.

DETROIT 1957

Stretched across my bed, I watched the neon lights blink on and off, off and on. The rhythm of the lights could really put you in a groove. Sometimes I'd even use that off and on rhythm to help me write my songs, and why not? I couldn't stop the damn things, so I might as well have used them.

I lived in a one-room apartment over Denny's Show Bar, off Linwood Avenue. It was not the best neighborhood by a long shot, but in those days, that's where all the action was. All the players, hookers, would-be's, could-be's and wannabe's were out in the streets every night from eight o'clock until three in the morning.

Denny's Show Bar was the hottest spot in the 'hood. Denny's featured the best local talent in Detroit. I'm talking about the hottest soul singing sistas and brothers in the city. Thursday through Sunday the place would be packed to the max, and man, was it loud. So you see I couldn't get any sleep even if I'd wanted to. Hell, I didn't need sleep anyway. What I needed was some money. I would just lie there waiting for the show to start. That week they were featuring Andre Williams and Gino Parks; two blues singin' fools.

From my apartment, positioned between just a few inches of wooden insulation directly over the stage, I could hear every word Andre and Gino sang and every note the band played. Now how's that for being in the thick of things? All that noise would probably have driven the average person crazy, but for me; a songwriter and singer, it was mother's milk, baby!

My room on Linwood was small but it held a lot of music; my tape recorder, my radio, and tucked in the corner, my soulful upright piano with a few missing strings and broken keys. It was slightly outta tune, but that's what gave it that funky sound, you feel me?

If I heard a song squeakin' through the floorboards, or something on the radio with a groove I liked, I would jump on the piano and start writing something from it. Man! I could bang away for hours, with nobody to stop me. I'd keep my tape recorder running, so when I heard something that really knocked me out, I would tape the music while I was singing and write myself a new song. Ahh, man! That was better than having your own karaoke band and background singers put together.

Boy, did I love it. Some of the songs I wrote back then became hits with Motown years later, but I'm getting ahead of myself.

Andre Williams and Gino Parks were really something. They were even better than me and Clarence Paul put together; literally. You see, I sang duet on a few dates with Clarence, who became a songwriter and producer at Motown. We were good, too, but we couldn't touch Andre Williams and Gino Parks. No way. Plus, there wasn't enough money in it for me. I watched Andre and Gino in rehearsal with my band a few times and I gotta tell you, I really liked em.' Yeah!

The band was hot, too. You see, I was the booker for most of the real funk musicians in the city. I'm talking about the musicians that the white agencies had absolutely no interest in. They wouldn't even consider them, even though the brothers could play their asses off.

These super talented musicians came to me for work and I got it for them. Some of them couldn't read music, but they could feel it and hear it. They could all read chords, and that was a good thing, because that's all you need when you're playing the blues. You only have three basic chords in the blues anyway - well, four if you take it to the bridge like James Brown used to scream at his JB's. I would get gigs for the brothers wherever music was needed; clubs, parties, celebrations of all kinds, in all the hottest after hour's joints in the city. The after-hours joints, now that's where they made good money!

An after-hours joint was the next generation's name for the speakeasy from the Roaring Twenties and the Days of Prohibition. Yes, the after-hours joints were illegal! Not a liquor license in sight, but the police and fire marshals had their reasons for looking the other way. As long as those niggas stayed in the ghetto with all that mess, it was all right with them. Sometimes those same cops would drop by the after hour's joints, pick up a plate of Southern fried chicken, some ribs, a handful of money, and they were outta there.

These joints started filling up as soon as people started leaving the local bars and house parties. You see, they weren't really ready to go home; they were ready to keep the party going. You had to know somebody to get in the after-hours joints and since everybody knew somebody, all the joints were packed at all times.

As soon as you walked in to any after-hours joint, you could smell the fried chicken, catfish, pig's feet, and barbecue ribs. If I close my eyes I can smell it right now. The aroma would knock your socks off. Hum! That Southern fried chicken was all crispy on the outside, tender & juicy on the inside. Give me a leg, a wing, and a thigh, with some Louisiana hot sauce on it and that was a taste to die for! And that catfish! Sprinkled with garlic salt and black pepper all rolled up in some of yellow cornmeal batter, deep-fried on both sides until it turned golden brown. That food would make you think you were in New Orleans, especially if you shook some Louisiana hot sauce on that bird. Pickled pig's feet never did anything for me. They say it's and acquired a taste. Well, I did not want to waste my time learning how to eat somebody's pig feet, you feel me? Some of my kinfolk from down South and their friends, however, loved them some pickled pig's feet. After three or four drinks, they'd start acting all crazy, dancin' and shoutin' and eatin' pig's feet like potato chips.

Now, when it came down to those barbecued ribs, that was another story altogether. It was the sauce! Even though the ribs were so tender they'd melt in your mouth, I'm tellin' you it was the sauce! How was it that every juke joint in Detroit knew how to make that delicious tastin' barbecue sauce? I'm talking about the kind that makes you pig out on ribs. In every joint, the ribs tasted and so smelled too good to be true, you know what I'm sayin'? I bet the same cook was running all over Detroit, from one after-hours joint to another, with the exact same sauce. Makin' money and havin' a good time doing it.

The music in the joint would be so hot and funky, everybody who came through the door would start poppin' their fingers and shakin' their ass, letting it all hang out. At the same time, they'd sing and shout their orders out.

"Give me some of that fried chicken, oh yeah, and some barbecued ribs, baby, and make the sauce hot! I like it hot!"

The funky music rode across the top of everything while the band played the hits of the day. You'd let your hair down dancing to that music. Everybody knew they could get anything and everything in the after-hours joint and if the proprietors didn't have it, they'd send out and get it for you. The ladies of the evening, dressed in their finest revealing outfits, would sit at the bar teasing the players, making them buy Champagne splits; that was the popular drink back in the day. In the back room, the dice were rollin' and the games were on. Like I said, the joint was jumpin'! I was known for getting the best gigs in the city for musicians and for getting the best money out of the club owners and after-hours joints, too. As part of the deal, the owners had to provide free drinks and all the catfish and fried chicken the band could eat. And since half the time it was the only meal they'd get that day, trust me when I say – They could eat!

The after-hours joint would give up the chicken, even the catfish sometimes; but free ribs? Well that was another thing altogether. In fact that was a no-no. You had to pay for the ribs – because like I said – musicians can EAT!

The club owners liked me because my bands and singers were always on time and sober. I had rules you had to follow and everybody – including the owners knew what they were. Rule number 1 – Don't be Late, Rule number 2 – Don't be High, Rule number 3 – You Will Pay Me My Commission! So we all got along and made a living, except I wasn't exactly living. I was babysitting a bunch of musicians and that's not what I wanted to spend my life doin'. Sometimes I would get down in my spirit and the blues would fall on me hard.

The blues always seemed to hit me around the same time, about 4:00 a.m. Four in the morning is the blues hour. Sinatra used to sing; It's a quarter to three, there's no one in the place except you and me...

Well, for us in Detroit, it was a quarter to four. The bars would be closed and the streets would almost be empty.

I'd look out of my window and watch some of the lonely people. The girls would try to catch another trick before they turned in. Drunks on the corner fighting over the last drop in a bottle cradled in torn paper bags. And then the street sweeper passing by and splashing water on them, as if they weren't even there. I'd holler out of the window at the truck driver,

"Hey! You bastard! You see them?" I knew he couldn't hear me, but I felt good anyway.

Then my mood would change and the blues would come down on me even harder. I'd get mad at myself for living like the way I was. Then I'd get out that bottle of mine, pour a glass of Courvoisier and roll up a joint of Acapulco-Gold.

That was the best weed in the city. Two or three deep, deep drags was all I needed to convince myself it was time to get the hell outta there. I've got to make more outta my life than this! I'd think to myself.

I'd bounce the thought around in my head until the Acapulco-Gold kicked in. Then I would take the tape recorder over to my funky old upright and I'd start writing a blues ballad to end all ballads. After playing it back on the tape recorder, I'd take another drink, another drag and start all over again. Thinking about ways to turn it all around, change everything, get away from this life of hustling, girls, drugs, you name it.

You see, in those days, I did it all. Some of the things I did because I wanted to. Some things I did because I knew no other way. I lived in Detroit, back in the day when street life was one of the ways to keep your head above the cesspool that was drowning so many Black people. Even if it didn't touch them physically, it was killing their spirits, their will to live and their self-esteem.

I'd see young Black men looking sixty years old when they were only thirty; especially those who worked in the automobile factories. Armies of Black people came up from the South just to work in those factories.

They got the jobs all right, working side by side with the white boys and getting paid a whole lot less money. Working long hours with no chance of getting equal pay, promotion, or a raise. If you complained you got fired, or worse, you might get your legs broken. Nobody talked about it much; you just had to find a way to live with it. You either lived in dilapidated housing, packed in like cattle and controlled by white slum-lords who were in cahoots with the courts, or you were on AFDC welfare (Aid to Families of Dependent Children) and lived in the projects.

The projects were the same then as they are now; a group of government buildings that house the disenfranchised in the poorest part of town. No project housing neighborhood was complete without a liquor store on every corner; where the owner would be kind enough to take your money, your food stamps, and, in some cases even your credit for booze.

Some of the folks in the neighborhood where I grew up had a weekly ritual. They'd work like crazy Monday through Thursday, get drunk as hell on Friday and on Saturday came the partyin', fightin', stabbin', and shootin'. Come Sunday morning they'd drag their butts to church, asking the Lord to forgive them for being such asses all weekend long. But as soon as the service was over, they'd hurry home from church to get to some baked chicken, dressing with greens and candied yams, turn on the TV, have sex, and make some more babies. Come Monday, it started all over again.

But not me; I decided at an early age, that whatever it took, I was not gonna work in nobody's factory or live in nobody's projects. So I ended up hustlin', gamblin', schemin' and dreamin'. I didn't live in the projects, and I didn't work in no factory either. I had a brand new 1957 Chevrolet Impala and my own little apartment. I didn't get drunk and raise hell... Well - that's not exactly true. I got a little drunk sometimes, a little high every now and then, and, like everybody else, I lived a life where I made some babies in the mix.

But we'll talk about all the kids later, not on this night, when the weed was good, the brandy went down easy, the music was good and my dreams were so big, I could see my songs at the top of every chart. All right, maybe not the country charts, but the R&B charts for sure. I knew there were better days ahead because there'd already been some great days in my life.

BROWN GAL

I was a kid when I performed at the famed Apollo Theater Amateur Night competition in Harlem, New York. My momma took me there.

My mom, Kitty "Brown Gal" Stevenson, was petite, brown, beautiful and strong as a single mother of four could be. Momma was a good entertainer, a wonderful singer/songwriter, and a bundle of rhythm and blues. Her children learned everything from her. I got my love of music right along with my mother's milk.

I was about eight when my mom started working with my brothers and me, grooming us as a singing trio. My brother Lonnie was seven and my baby brother Martin was five. Momma always wanted us to be in show business. She was performing in New York - I think it was at Small's Paradise; a famous nightclub in Harlem. In those days, Small's, played artists like Dinah Washington, Brook Benton, the Sweethearts of Rhythm, the Ravens, the Orioles, and other Black artists.

My mom knew the guy who ran the amateur shows at the Apollo. Somehow she got him to put me and my brothers on as contestants. By that time, I was about ten and my brother Lonnie was nine. Martin, my baby brother, was almost seven and could out "sang" all of us. He was very, very shy and nervous. How he got that way I have no idea, but because of his problem Momma would rehearse us relentlessly. The more you rehearse the more it becomes a part of you, and you will react without thinking about it. That's what Momma said; and guess what? Momma was right!

I even remember the song we were going to sing, though I don't recall the title. Its lyrics included the words "Baby, when I found you..."

We had a gimmick at the end of the song too. My little brother would drop down on one knee and sing "Baby, baby, when I found you!"

It always drew a big laugh and lots of applause.

The night of the contest, all contestants had to go through the Apollo's stage entrance on 126th Street. The backstage stair case seemed narrower than it was, with what felt like a thousand people constantly running up and down the steps all the time.

11

ve.

Standing in the curtains backstage was this funny-looking guy, dressed in a clown's uniform and holding a long hook. He was easily over six feet tall and the hook was taller than he was. He was standing just out of sight of the singer who was performing onstage.

The singer, sad to say, was terrible! She made everyone cringe when she hit the bad notes - and she was singing a lot of bad notes. You could hear people in the audience yelling some terrible things at that poor woman,

"Boo! Get off the stage! Sandman! Sandman!"

All of a sudden - Sandman, the strange fella in the clown outfit - ran onstage with his long hook and hooked it around the neck of the singer. Dancing all the way; he yanked and yanked her until they both disappeared offstage. The audience went crazy! My brothers and I stood frozen.

Seeing the look on our faces, my mom whispered, "Don't worry, the Sandman won't do that to you."

Terrified of the hook coming for us, when it was our turn to sing, we sang our butts off. My baby brother was usually shy and nervous, but when it was time for his solo he dropped down on both knees like he was praying. His voice was so loud and clear he shocked everybody!

"Baby, baby when I found you-o-o-o..."

The audience went wild! We WON! We WON! First place! My momma never stopped smiling at her babies. The memory of her happiness made that song very special to me. If anyone knows the song and its title, it would be an act of kindness to post it on my website www.facebook.com/williammickeystevenson.

Kitty Stevenson was in demand. She sang with the great Todd Rhodes and his orchestra. Man, she was good! She had to be; she supported and took care of four kids and a grandmother all by herself. She paid every bill and kept food on our table. We were not on welfare; no Aid to Families of Dependent Children or food stamps for Kitty "Brown Gal" Stevenson's kids.

Momma never had a big hit record, yet she was known as one of the best R&B singers ever. Just a few years ago, I got a surprise letter and package from a blues collector in England, saying how great Momma was.

He even sent me some songs of hers that I had never heard. Now that's really saying something.

Momma came home one day all excited, telling us kids about this crazy young six feet something, handsome as-he-wanna-be, cab driver who would pick her up every night from the club and bring her home for free. His name was Ted Moore. She called him Teddy. Ted first saw my mom singing at the Famous Flame Show Bar. It was Detroit's equivalent to Harlem's notorious Cotton Club, where the best dancers, singers, and comics came to perform in the city. Some of the other artists who performed there were Dinah Washington, Joe Williams and Sarah Vaughan. The club's orchestra was conducted by the renowned Maurice King, a wonderful classical arranger and conductor, very proper and sophisticated. He was well-known as a conductor and arranger during World War II, for taking a multiracial, all-female orchestra called the Sweethearts of Rhythm, on tour to replace the big bands whose men had gone to war. Maurice was a big man with a lot of class and had a few strands of gray hair left on his head that matched his white tie and tails. Even his shoes were white. Maurice King would end up back in my life when I was a grown man.

Teddy, the cab driver, wouldn't let anybody give my momma a ride home. When he found out she had four kids, he would not only bring her home for free but he'd give her a handful of money, probably most of the money he made driving his cab all week. That was Ted.

Ted was not only tall and good-looking he was built like a gladiator; with the biggest hands I ever saw. He was younger than Mom. When they were together he looked more like her younger brother than a love sick adult, and I do mean love sick. Man, was he hooked! It's what you call crazy in love. His dream came true about six months later when he and my momma got married. Talk about your epic love stories. You should have seen his face. You couldn't hack the smile off his face with a chisel. Ted Moore was like a kid who had just found his own candy store. Momma didn't smoke, drink, or curse. She was very kind and gentle. To me, she was more than just my mother, she was my friend. I could tell her anything and everything, and I did. She was fine, like we used to say in the neighborhood. I mean real fine in every way. She had character and beauty.

When the cancer came down on her, she was only twenty-eight years old. She went from 128 pounds to eighty pounds. While she was in Memorial Hospital, she reached a point where she was so weak, she was unable to speak. She had to blink her eyes yes or no. As I watched

Momma trying to ring the bell for the nurse, stretching her fingers as far as she could, I grabbed her hand. With my other hand, I pushed the button. Momma smiled at me and blinked her eyes Yes. When the nurse came to help Momma go to the bathroom, all I could think about was; who was gonna ring the bell for her the next time? When visiting hours were over and everyone would leave her room, I'd duck under the bed and wait until the nurse turned out the lights. Then I'd crawl out to let Momma know I was there. She'd look at me with her big, pretty, teary eyes, and I swear I could see them smiling at me. I'd smile back at her and hold the smile on my face as long as I could and then I'd duck under the bed again so she wouldn't see me crying.

When Momma died, I couldn't cry or nothing. I'd done all my crying under her bed while she lay dying. I would just think about her smiling eyes. Then I'd get mad. How could God let someone so important to me go out like that? I gotta tell you, I was mad at God for a long, long time.

Ted, my poor stepfather, fell apart. He started drinking and crying every night. It was hard to watch him suffer like that. He was losing it. Teddy had to leave; he had to get away from the place where he was the happiest, luckiest man on earth. He had to find himself before it was too late. He couldn't take care of any teenagers. He couldn't take care of himself.

With Momma up in heaven, my brothers and I - The Stevenson Trio - just lost interest in performing. We sang together for a few more years, doing amateur shows and contests off and on. We won most of them too. But without Momma it wasn't the same. We slowly lost interest in performing as a group.

Grand-momma Roxy took over to try and hold the family together. And guess what? We ended up on welfare and some other government programs. I hated getting those government Christmas goodwill packages full of white underwear, cheese, butter, and beans. My sister and brothers could handle it, but not me. All I could think of was, my mother's pride, how she had been able to take such good care of us– with no welfare in the way.

TIME FLIES

I was thirteen going on thirty when Momma left me. I was too old and too hurt to be supervised by anyone. I just decided to do my own thing and my thing was to make money —no welfare for me. From the ages of thirteen through sixteen, I was in and out of juvenile hall so much that the head jailer knew my name on sight.

"Hey Mickey!" he'd say, "Get your uniform, toiletries and find your bed. You know the routine."

The last time I got busted, it was for breaking and entering. Oh yeah - and stealing a cop's car. Even I knew I was in serious trouble that time. The judge released me in Momma Roxy's care until the trial date. I decided not to wait. I slipped away and joined the Air Force. I had to lie about my age since I was only sixteen and a half, but with the help of Momma Roxy, nobody found out. I found a home in the Air Force and really thought seriously about making a career of it. I was in the special unit that organized entertainment. I'd get singers, dancers and musicians to perform and I got pretty good at it too.

But everything changed when I came home on furlough. I went to see a show at the old Warfield Theater. It was more than our neighborhood theater; it was our Apollo, like the Regal Theater in Chicago and the Uptown in Baltimore. Some of those theaters were turned into churches when their heydays were over, but while the theaters were up and running, baby, you got to see a big recording star, an amateur show, a movie and a cartoon, all for a dollar and a half!

Detroit always had good artists and the Warfield was the outlet for the up and coming Black artists. One night I attended a show there and was really enjoying myself watching the crowd and the amateurs in their colorful outfits, competing with each other.

After watching three or so acts that were good, but not great, an act came on called the Four Aims; four tall, sharp brothers with waves in their hair. They wore shiny gray mohair suits with ties and shoes to match. And to kick it off, they wore a kind of open collar shirt called a "Mr. B," after the great Billy Eckstine.

15

These brothers could sang, not sing; I know what I said, I said sang! You got it? They won the amateur show hands down. They sang the blues with some jazz and rock & roll - all rolled up in the same song, called Rock, Roll. They were fantastic! I thought to myself, these guys are going places!

I listened to the crowd applauding and screaming. You could feel the energy in the air. I thought about my mother, about singing with my brothers at The Apollo Theater. I let the music and the feeling wash over me and right then and there, I made up my mind - This is going to be my life. This is the business I wanna be in!

As soon as I got back to the base I told my commanding officer I was not going to re-up. He didn't like it much. He tried to convince me that I would make a fine officer, a good leader for my people and all that. But I was sold on the music business and nothing was gonna change my mind. The world of music and entertainment was the road I was going to take.

The Four Aims helped change my life. Down the road, I was able to help change their lives, too.

Show business had me hooked. I cut the Air Force loose thinking I'd get right into it once I shook the uniform dust off my shoes. My siblings had grown up during my time in the Air Force. My sister Elaine had two kids, my brother Lonnie was in college studying acting or something like that. My baby brother Martin, the shy one who would drop to his knees and sing, became an MP in the Army. He was known for breaking heads and taking no prisoners, can you believe it? Man, how things had changed.

Along the way, I had picked up a family of my own. My first son, Mickey, Jr., was about a year old and Craig, son number two, was still in the oven. When you first get out of the service and come home, you get happy and all you wanna do is party down. You're out spending money and having a ball. Well, I'm not gonna lie about it; that's just what I did. But I soon found out that snagging a job as a singer/songwriter in Detroit was impossible. Finding any job that was worthwhile was easier said than done. I was aware of the automobile plants, but once you planted your feet in those auto factories, it was like being married until death do us part. And that was not for me, no way.

My Air Force pay had run out. I was stone cold broke, and being broke don't work with a wife and two kids. As for me, I want you to know that I couldn't stand getting handouts from anybody; especially the government. I put my music career on hold, passed up the auto plants and decided to get back to what I knew worked; hustling and working the streets, cards, girls, gambling, whatever.

TWO OLD FRIENDS

Just as I was getting started, I ran into two old friends from my high school days, Joe Miles and Elliott Gabriel. We used to sing together from the days of middle school right up to Northeastern High. We called ourselves the Meadow Larks. We were good, too! I mean good with a capital G. We wore cocoa brown suits with Mister B shirts and cocoa brown shoes. Every time we sang, Sixty Minute Man, by the Ravens, it was over! We'd do a couple quick dance steps, spin around, drop down on one knee (which worked every time), and start singing.

"If your man ain't treat'n you right, Come on and take my hand I'll rock you, roll you, all night long 'Cause I'm your sixty minute man, yeah, yeah, yeah."

All the girls would go crazy! We were so cool that we got invited to sing at all the school parties and house parties, you name it. The Meadow Larks were gettin' down! I did most of the lead singing so I got all the girls, of course. That's why most young guys get into show business to begin with - that's the truth.

Joe and Gabriel had a job coming up singing as The Hamptones, with the great Lionel Hampton. They were a man short. Their lead singer left them high and dry for another group. They were gonna lose the job if they didn't come up with another lead singer, and quick. They asked me if I was interested. Who you kiddin'? I jumped at it. I let my wife know I was going on the road for a while and not to worry. I'd send her some money as soon as I got it. We left the next day.

I couldn't believe it. It was like a dream come true. One minute I couldn't find a job worth nothin' and the next minute, I'm the lead singer for the Hamptones on the road with the great Lionel Hampton! He was a jazz vibraphonist, pianist, percussionist, bandleader and actor. Hampton ranks among the great names in jazz history; he worked with everybody from Benny Goodman and Charlie Parker to Buddy Rich and Quincy Jones. Now is God good, or what?

The tour with Lionel and his band was an eye-opener for me on many levels. Lionel's wife, Gladys Hampton, ran the whole show, and she ran it harder than anything I ever saw in the military. She was short and thin but she walked and talked like she was six feet tall and in charge. Watching her work with all of those different personalities and the way she held that whole show together, moving us from place to place, was truly a sight to behold. I learned a lot from her about musicians and artists, their temperament, their personalities, their insecurities and above all, how to gain their loyalty and respect.

She even put a manager with us. His name was Welton E. Barnett. He was as slick and as smooth as they came. Barnett looked like he was from someplace in Europe. He was very thin; about five feet five with a well-trimmed, low cut beard and beady eyes. He was a health food nut and could always be found eating something. The man was always well dressed; his hat matched the coat he wore like a cape draped over his shoulders like a foreigner. I don't know where he was from, but I'm willing to bet that brother was born in Alabama somewhere. I do know this; he took 20 percent of our money for doing absolutely nothing, and he could do nothing very well. To this day I believe he gave Gladys a 10 percent kickback for giving him the group to manage, but that didn't really matter. Welton E. was good! I learned a lot from him, too. We played the best rooms in the country, from New York to California.

The tour was great, until we hit Las Vegas, where we were not allowed to enter the casino area at all - no gambling, no nothing, and don't even think it. Imagine what that was like for Lionel Hampton, who was as big a star as Benny Goodman and other big bands of that era.

He had appeared in the movies with them and everything, but he couldn't go into the casino area, not even to the bathroom. That was too deep for me! I thought the war was over. Boy, was I naïve. I had a lot to learn and the lessons were on the way. The hotel managers in Las Vegas weren't dumb enough to put up signs saying "No Niggers Allowed," but the treatment was the same as if we had been in Lynchburg, Virginia, or somewhere in the USA with blinking neon signs ten feet tall;

NO NIGGERS ALLOWED AT ALL

We couldn't stay in the hotel or even walk through the lobby. We entered and exited the hotel through the kitchen. Our rooms were located on the other side of town - they called it The Dust Bowl. Black folks could perform on the Strip, park the cars, clean the rooms, mop floors, wash the dishes, even cook the food (that was a joke if you get my drift) but when you finished your job; don't hang around the hotels or the casinos. The running gag was I wouldn't wanna be you, if they see you.

Of course we'd lived with racism all of our lives, but I was still fresh outta the Air Force. For an ex-soldier who could fight for you, maybe even die for you, but wasn't allowed to live around you or even go to the same bathroom as you, it was hard to stomach.

Can you feel me?

THE MOULIN ROUGE

And then came the game changer - a hotel built just for us.

The Moulin Rouge opened on May 24, 1955, built at a cost of $3.5 million, which was really a lot of money back then. The hotel was located in the dust bowl, West Las Vegas, where the Black population lived. West Las Vegas was bounded by Washington Avenue on the north, Bonanza Road on the south, H Street on the west and A Street on the east. The Brown Bomber, Joe Lewis, owned part of the place, but the other guys who owned it were Jewish or Italian.

The Moulin Rouge was the first desegregated hotel and casino. It was a hot spot for all the Black entertainers of that time; the known and the hoping to be known. It served as a safe haven for Black artists who were allowed to perform at the neighboring hotels and casinos yet not allowed to enjoy benefits from their stay like the crowds of people they were hired to entertain. Most of the Black artists who packed them in at the hotels and casinos on the Strip had to stay in The Dust Bowl. They were either housed in the Moulin Rouge or they stayed in the little motel right across the street. If both were booked up, they had better find someone to room and board with, or they were shit outta luck.

That place - even the name Moulin Rouge--was really special. The casino walls framed life-sized original paintings of great Black artists singing, dancing, or playing instruments. The paintings were in bright, vibrant colors that made the portrait of each artist seem to come to life. On June 20, 1955, Life Magazine put the place on its cover, with two showgirls strutting so hard they seemed to jump off the page. It wasn't just the showgirls who were great looking. All the waitresses there had great legs; I would have bet anybody that they were all handpicked for their legs. They knew how to pour a brother a real drink, too!

The Moulin Rouge had a showroom that held about five hundred people and a nice sized stage that could accommodate a full band with room for the singers and dancers. There were stars everywhere. The place was so packed that they eventually had to add a third show every night. Inevitably at some point in the evening the crowd would eventually double in attendance! It was where you'd find stars like Sammy Davis, Jr., Frank Sinatra, Dean Martin, the whole Rat Pack, and more. Everybody who was anybody would leave the strip when their shows were over and bring their parties down to The Dust Bowl, straight to The Moulin Rouge. It was like a casino after-hours joint for the stars; the rich and famous. The stars could feel free to have a good time there, no press, no mess; they could be themselves and nobody cared. Sometimes there were more white folks there than Blacks; all having the time of their lives. The music was hot, the chorus girls were sexy and they could dance their asses off. Sammy, Sinatra, and the Rat Pack would go onstage with the band and the girls and have a ball.

For a while it was said that the hotel was owned by the first African American woman to hold a Nevada gaming license, Sarann Knight-Preddy. Now I don't know personally the part she played in bringing that place to life, but one thing for certain is, the Moulin Rouge was the spark needed to bring an end to segregation on the Las Vegas Strip. The Moulin Rouge got to be so popular it worried the big club owners on the strip. Mysteriously, it went bankrupt and later there was an arson fire. That was the bad news. The good news was that after the Moulin closed, the NAACP started making more noise and so did the powerhouse Black entertainers, like Lena Horne.

In 1960, under threat of a planned protest march against Racial Discrimination in Las Vegas Casinos, that was designed to march straight down the Las Vegas Strip, a meeting was arranged between hotel owners, city and state officials, local Black leaders, and the NAACP. The meeting held on March 26th at the closed Moulin Rouge, resulted in an agreement to desegregate all Las Vegas Strip casinos. I remember talking to Sammy Davis, Jr., about how we felt the night we walked right through the front door of the Sands Hotel and nobody told us we couldn't!

What a night. Las Vegas was changed forever.

LONG ROAD HOME

The tour with Lionel Hampton didn't last long enough for me. I learned a lot and did a lot and I was sorry when it was over. We ended the tour on the West Coast. Nobody in our group wanted to go home, so we let Barnett, our manager, talk us into working some shows in Los Angeles.

We played our first gig at the 5/4 Ballroom, opening the show for Hank Ballard & The Midnighters. Hank was from Detroit too, and was known all over the R&B world for his funky sexy recordings of Work with Me Annie and the follow up to it, Annie Had A Baby (She Can't Work No Mo). It was one of those tunes that made everybody laugh while they danced their butts off. Etta James' cleaned up version of the same damn song, Dance with Me Henry, got her a big hit. But Hank and his guys came back with the original version of Gladys Knight's first hit, Every Beat of My Heart. Hank kicked it up a notch when he invented the dance and wrote the song, The Twist. That song took him into the pop market, and that's the song the whole world was dancing to after Chubby Checker re-recorded it and renamed it Come On Baby, Let's Do The Twist! The 5/4 Ballroom was a far cry from the great rooms we played with the Hampton organization. That was the upscale end of music venues. This was the other end of that scale. First of all, it was located on 54th and Broadway in Los Angeles. In those days, that was pretty deep in the heart of the ghetto. The 5/4 ballroom was located upstairs. You had to walk up a narrow staircase of thirty-three steps; I counted them every night. It was so narrow only two people could pass at a time, one going up and one coming down to where the food was.

The doorman was a huge Black brother with two missing teeth right in the front; and that brother weighed over three hundred pounds. He looked very intimidating in his torn white T- shirt with the face of a bulldog on it. The brother was no one to fool around with. He stopped everybody at the top of the stairs and patted them down for knives, razors, guns, and ice picks. Many of the women carried razors and icepicks. You could tell he loved patting the girls down by the big smile on his face as he felt, touched and squeezed everything.

Hair, tits, ass, you name it, he touched it and loved it. There were plenty of weapons being tossed in the big red box by the door, too. When you entered the Ballroom, the heat would knock you down. The 5/4 ballroom was dark, hot, thick with a heady mix of body odor and cheap cologne.

When you finally adjusted your eyes to the light, and your nose to the scents you found yourself looking at 500 or more people jammed in the place, drinking, sweating, and dancing to the funky music, bumping and grinding away. Some of them would be holding each other so tight you couldn't separate them with a bucket of ice water. I had a chance to see and learn what the other side of the music world was like; the soulful side, the real rhythm and blues side. I'm talking about the funky blues side with the funky hotel rooms and the watered down booze.

As soon as the shows were over, everybody who was anybody would head straight to the Adams Hotel. That's where all the entertainers stayed, including us. Everybody went straight to the bar because that's where the real party was going on; singing, dancing, and gettin' down to the sounds of some great musicians. I'm talking about musicians who could play everything from classical and jazz to rhythm and blues. They came to the hotel party from every show and night club in town. They brought all their different personalities and attitudes along with them. You can learn a lot about an artist in that atmosphere. Some artists have inflated egos and insecurities and need to surround themselves with go-fers and yes-men, who said yes sir and no sir on cue. Then there were the artists who couldn't stand being alone; they had their so-called friends who attach themselves to whoever is spending the most money, buying gifts, dinners, and drinks. Artists, musicians, hangers-on, everybody came to have fun, hang out and talk trash. The groupies were all there with tight short skirts and sexy high heels and very willing attitudes. I learned about this kinda stuff first hand, and what a lesson it was. You never knew who you'd see, doing whatever in this world, with whomever.

Barnett, our so-called manager, had quite an imagination. This guy would book us in some pretty wild places. But it was work, and we needed it. The straw that broke the camel's back was when he booked us in a Mexican theater in downtown L.A. It was an all-Mexican show.

You read it right! An all-Mexican show where everyone spoke Spanish except us! On top of that, he told us that the show paid a certain rate, and we found out it paid over a thousand dollars more. That did it! We parted company and I became the group's manager. We all agreed to hang in L.A. and try to get some more work. We found a one-room apartment that had a pull-out bed and an old upright piano. What a blessing that was! The bed could only hold one person, though, so the three of us took turns sleeping on it. I got us some studio work singing background and overdubbing for pop and rock artists. We were good, so the jobs came faster and they got better.

We got lucky when we did some background work early in 1957 for a singer who was the original "Bob" in the duo Bob & Earl. His name was Bobby Day and we ended up working with him. I call him The Three Hit Wonder! He recorded three songs that became rock and roll classics to this day; Over & Over, Little Bitty Pretty One, and Rockin' Robin. His manager asked us to go on the tour with Bobby as The Satellites. This was a totally different kinda tour from anything I'd done before. There were new lessons to be learned. It was my first introduction to the Southern Circuit. It was different from the Chitlin' Circuit up north, and a thousand light years from the kind of tour I'd done with Lionel Hampton.

This was a tour that went to the largest Black-populated, unheard-of cities and towns in the South. We worked in cubby holes with sawdust on the floor and fights every night; where the blues was king, the food was great, and the singers had better know how to sing or they would get something thrown upside their heads. You worked all night and you drove all day. And you fought with the promoters for your money along the way. On this tour, I had to work with a different band almost every night. That was pretty regular for singers with hits. They got pick-up bands that knew the hit songs, and it cut out a lot of the expense of travel and hotels. Chuck Berry did it exactly that way for fifty years. He would fly into town the day of the gig, maybe do a sound check, maybe not; but he figured if you didn't know at least ten Chuck Berry hits, you shouldn't call yourself a musician; and he was right.

Bobby Day, like all too many artists, had a love affair with the booze. He could put away a fifth of Old Granddad Whiskey like it was water. The brother would drink a glassful before going onstage, and by the time we were into the second song he would be drunk as a skunk. But Bobby could still sang the taste out your mouth; he wouldn't miss a note. Sometimes we had to hold him up to the mic so he wouldn't fall, while we sang the background and did the dance routine, all at the same time.

Man! There ain't enough money in the world to go through all that again. After that tour we were all ready to go home. We had some money and I had had enough of this road stuff. The whole trip was quite an experience. It was added to my lessons of learning this business called show business. Being cheated out of ownership of songs you wrote, getting ripped off by publishers, promoters, and record companies. Artists being used like commodities by managers. Working jive ass joints with some jive ass people. And the list goes on. But then there was the other side of show business; working with great artists, the wonderful show rooms and fine hotels, learning about production shows and musicians, experiencing what self-control, loyalty, and respect really meant. Meeting many people in this world of entertainment, who are truly gifted; some endowed with exceptional gifts, others with skill, class and charisma. And of course a whole lot of them are gifted with a lotta bullshit! And the bullshit flies on both sides of the fence. Maybe the most important thing I learned was about myself - I discovered that I was a better leader than I was a follower. Learning and then making informed decisions based on that information made me a confident leader. Leading, felt like a custom tailored suit - and that was a very good lesson to learn about myself.

Working our way back to Detroit, we picked up this singer, Paula...uh, I can't remember her last name, I believe it was Greer. No, that's not it... that was the girl in Chicago. Anyway, I remember Paula had a big voice and looked like Sarah Vaughan. She was short, beautiful dark skin, with big lips and big hips. She acted like Sarah Vaughan, too. The girl could sing some jazz. We worked mostly jazz clubs with acts like the Four Aces, the High Lows, Lambert, Hendricks, Ross & Bevan, and some other jazz groups. We held our own.

I gotta tell you, to me singing jazz has to be a calling; a mission if you will! Now don't get me wrong. I really liked singing jazz because it had a much more relaxed pace. But it wasn't paying off for me. The other members of the group loved it. If it had been up to them, we would have stayed out there riding the jazz riffs forever. Personally, I was up to my neck with performing onstage and on the road, period! I wanted to get home to be with my wife and kids. I really missed them. Nobody else in the group had any kids or a wife, so we were not all on the same page, you know what I mean?

LADY SINGS THE BLUES

When I hit Detroit, I had a bouquet of roses in my hand and a smile on my face. I opened the door to my apartment, anxious to see my wife and kids; instead I walked into a surprise. My wife and her momma had been waiting for me.

Elizabeth Wright (a real mother-in-law, if you know what I mean) was standing there with her arms folded and with an attitude on her face. My mother- in-law started right in on me.

"I hope you're through with all this foolishness; running around the country with a bunch of songbirds." She turned to her daughter. "Go on and tell him what we talked about, baby."

Betty Ann, looking exactly like her momma, folded her arms and charged right in.

"I can't live like this anymore. You're gonna have to get a regular job like everybody else."

Wow! I was thinking to myself. What happened to that sweet, innocent demeanor my wife had when I left?

Her momma started tapping her foot.

"I think you better make up your mind right now, Mister Sanger! What is it gonna be?"

I smiled when I told her, "I think you need to take six months to mind your own business, and another six months to leave grown folks alone. Now will you get outta my house?"

"Your house?" she snapped back, "What house? This apartment is as much my daughter's as it is yours." She proceeded to sit down in what used to be my favorite chair and cross her legs.

"And I ain't goin' anywhere."

My wife, looking more and more like her momma every minute, sat down in the other chair and crossed her legs too!

"If she leaves, I'm leaving!"

I took a long look at both of them and I didn't like what I saw. I could tell the daughter was going to keep changing until she was exactly like her momma. That was not my idea of a partner for life. I needed some time to think this thing over. It took about three seconds.

"Baby," I said, "instead of your momma leaving, you and your momma can stay here with each other. I'm leaving!"

And I walked out.

Not long after that confrontation with her momma, my wife said her feelings for me had changed. I could understand because my feelings for her had changed too.

Meanwhile, she and the kids moved in with her momma and I moved into the vacant apartment over Denny's Show Bar with those rhythmic blinking lights outside my window. It didn't take long before a divorce was in the mix. And that, as they say, was the end of that.

MUSICAL CHAIRS

It was time to visit Benny Mullins - the best process barber in the city. When Benny straightened your hair and put his half-inch finger waves on your head, baby your hair would stand up at least three inches from your scalp, and the waves could rock a battleship! It was pretty.

Benny had all the players, hustlers and wannabes as his customers. Anybody who even thought they were somebody got their hair processed, waved and set at Benny Mullins' House of Styles on 12th Street.

The barber shop was laid out in red and black colors. Even the chairs were red and black. But the coolest thing was the big picture window right in front. You could be seen by all the ladies who passed by, while you were getting your hair laid out at Benny's. And if you were looking for someone, you could see if they were in the shop as well. Late at night, when some of the Black stars were in town and a hot clothes sale was going down courtesy of two of the biggest boosters in the city - I'm talking about Baby Doll and Dorothy Helena - Benny would close the big red window curtains and lock all the doors.

Even though there were only two barbers in the place, the shop was always jam-packed. It had two dryers and four barber chairs. Benny had a system that worked. It was like musical chairs; Benny and the other barber each had a customer in one chair waiting, while they worked on a customer in the other chair and stashed two people under the dryers. Everybody else had to find something to do until it was their turn. There were guys talking in the two payphone booths, guys playing chess, others playing dominos, and the rest telling regular barber shop lies.

Thank God! It was my turn in the chair. As I sat down, I looked at the guy in the chair next to me getting his hair processed. Benny introduced us. Benny liked the idea of putting people together in his shop. Once you got involved in conversation, it took your mind off the fact that you had been in his shop for hours.

"Berry Gordy, Mickey Stevenson. Mickey, Berry."

As we shook hands, Berry Gordy said he had heard about me and was glad to meet me. He told me he was starting his own record company and he would like to have a meeting with me when he got back from Chicago. He

31

was going there to finish working with Jackie Wilson.

Jackie Wilson!? He was one of my favorite artists! This was exciting to know. Jackie Wilson was technically the best R&B-soul singer of his lifetime. He had it all; range, power, control, and the ability to bend and stretch any syllable into a long string of notes, faster, smoother and longer than anyone. He was handsome, and dressed to the max. Jackie would have been amazing if he'd just planted his feet on the ground and sung. But he did way more than that. While singing full steam, Jackie would do double spins, hurl the mic into the air, drop down into the splits while he caught the mic and start singing notes nobody else could reach. Man! I had some songs that I wanted that brother to hear. I kept my excitement under control.

"So you're working with Jackie Wilson?" I asked, cool and polite.

Berry was even cooler with his answer. "Yeah, I'm writing some new songs for his album."

Benny Mullins jumped in while putting some money in the juke box. "Berry wrote some of Jackie's biggest hits, including this one you like, Mickey."

At that moment, To Be Loved was playing on the juke box. That's when I lost all that cool I'd been faking.

"To Be Loved!" I blurted out. "That's my jam! It's the hottest R&B record in the country, baby!"

Berry looked at me, the smallest of smiles hovering around his mouth. The song was a hit and Jackie was one of the first Black recording artists to cross over to pop airplay. But Berry and I had to stop talking; two dryers had just become available. You gotta understand; when a hair dryer was ready at Benny's place, you better grab it or you'd be standing around for another three hours, and that's the truth!

As Berry and I went under the hair dryers, we exchanged numbers. While under the dryer, I started thinking about the time I saw Jackie Wilson at the Warfield Theater. Jackie was big in Detroit. He was not just another singer to us Detroiters. Oh no, he was much more than that! Jackie was a player, a lover, the kingpin with all the ladies. Whenever he was at the Warfield, it was packed with the hottest chicks from all over. It was standing room only. The night I went to see Jackie, there were players and girls there who'd come all the way from Toledo, Ohio, to see him.

Everybody was dressed to the bone, looking good. Some girls had on outfits so tight they could hardly walk. They must've rubbed some baby oil all over their bodies so they could slide into some of those outfits. You could tell it was baby oil because their legs had the same shine as their arms and cleavage. All the dresses were so tight and short that a brother's imagination would have him running to the bathroom just to cool down. When Jackie hit the stage, the girls started screaming ...

"Mickey, Mickey, Mickey! Wake up, man, your hair is dry. I need this dryer."

Benny was shaking me, waking me up from a deep sleep. Berry Gordy was gone, and I had fallen asleep, which was easy to do under the hair dryer. As I walked out of the shop with my hair laid out, I thought, Wow, I just met Berry Gordy. I was on a roll, and anything could happen now. And it did. I was crazy happy walking to my car, when out of nowhere a pack of cop cars surrounded me. Cops swarmed out of the cars with their guns drawn. They grabbed me and slammed me onto the hood of the car. I was under arrest for extortion, racketeering, and sale of narcotics; heroin to be specific. Cocaine was around during that time, but that was for the rich and famous. Heroin! That was for fools, junkies and poor folks who didn't have enough sense to leave drugs alone.

My mind was racing. It was all a lie! I was no extortionist or racketeer. None of that crap! The only thing I ever dealt was a deck of cards. The truth was that Junior, one of the musicians who worked for me, didn't wanna pay me my commission, and he had been bragging about not paying me, so I had to take advantage of a bad situation by making an example of him. I had to fix it so that nobody else would even think about not paying me for my services, in other words, holding out on me. You see what I'm sayin'? I had a couple of brothers pay Junior a little visit, and they gently persuaded him to give me all of my money. To make a long story short, he was the one who had made up all those lies about me and told his aunt who worked for the police department that I was racketeering and whatever. Now, I wasn't adored by the police in the first place, given my juvenile activities and my somewhat misunderstood reputation. My God, I had just met Berry Gordy and I was going to jail.

GET OUTTA JAIL FREE CARD

When they threw me in the back of the police car, I kept thinking of my kids. I took good care of them, and just like my mother, I swore that no child of mine would ever be on any government subsidy. So that's why I had to get knee deep in my hustle--booking gigs, charging the musicians a percentage and the club owners, too. I had mouths to feed.

I always got my money one way or another. Only this time the boys had to persuade Junior to pay me my money. As I said, his aunty worked with the police department, and she pulled up all my past records, including my joining the Air Force while in my grandmother's custody. It didn't take much encouragement for the cops to lock me up. Even though the charges wouldn't hold water, it still gave the prosecutor a chance to railroad me.

But I got lucky! It was during the time I was being booked by the police. It seems one of the police officers, a captain, was interested in show business. He and his partner were involved in a record company. They owned a few labels, but the main line was HOB Records; a gospel label. They needed a producer, and somehow the captain got the idea that I could be that person. He gave me a "get outta jail free card"; a job with HOB Records, producing and writing songs.

The captain's associate and friend was the entrepreneur Carmen Caver Murphy, owner of HOB Records and founder of the House of Beauty. The House of Beauty was a beauty and charm school attended by some of the finest Black girls in the city. Miss Murphy and the police captain made a good team. I had never met a lady like Miss Murphy. I had never even seen a lady like her except in the movies. She was tall, very tall, and regal, like English royalty, a duchess or a countess, someone like that. She had long, beautiful hair that was slightly gray around the edges, and it complemented her face. She had that Georgia peach complexion, and her smile was an invitation to friendship.

Now I gotta tell ya - the only thing I really knew about gospel music was; The Five Blind Boys, and Mahalia Jackson - with her amazing contralto voice. Oh yea! And pretty hot looking Della Reese was making some noise in the gospel area. Beyond that I was pretty much in the dark.

Sure I went to church with Momma when I was a kid, like most Black kids, and I was eager to get outta there when the service was over, also like most Black kids. In Momma's church, traditional hymns and spirituals were the songs of the day. But outside of the church and in the streets, a whole new sound in religious music was developing. Miss Murphy's HOB Records broke the ice when it released the first album by James Cleveland's choir, The Voices. The Love of God made history, and that made HOB Records a force to be reckoned with. James Cleveland, the producer better known as The King of Gospel, established The Voices as one of the most versatile choirs in the country. With producers and artists like Cleveland, The Staples Singers, Aretha Franklin and a host of other singers and songwriters expressing themselves, gospel music took on a new life.

Common belief is that Black singers learned what they know from singing in Black churches - because everybody in the Black church can sing. Wrong! They got some terrible singers in some of these churches. So that belief is only partially true. Hey! There are singers right now, singing this Sunday morning in somebody's church, who can out-sing most of the people on the charts. And they're not just in the Black church; you can take that to the bank.

When the captain tapped me on the shoulder and asked me to do this gospel thing, it had been a long time since I had had one foot inside a church. When Momma died in that hospital with me hiding under her bed, I was really through with church, God, and everything else religious, for that matter. And I didn't want to hear about it either. Now I ask you, what kind of twist of fate was it that I ended up, years later, writing and producing records for a gospel label? The extra twist was that the most beautiful girls in Detroit were interested in singing for Jesus. Working with the girls, the label, writing and producing gospel songs, man! I enjoyed every minute of it. I walked out of jail and went straight to heaven - and that's The Gospel Truth!

The captain and I got to be real good friends. Can you imagine me being friends with a cop? I would even hang out and have lunch with him and wouldn't care who saw us together, either. With my get outta jail free card, I could go to the after-hours joints without worrying about getting busted. I could work my musicians with the club owners, smoke a little weed, play a little poker, whatever. As long as I didn't take things too far, I had it made!

With the captain as my friend, now and then he'd say something and I'd hear something that would come in handy; like the time he mentioned a booster the cops were looking for. This booster was a good friend of mine. A booster is one who steals designer clothes from the finest stores in the city. It was a true art. Baby Doll, who was my friend and one of the finest boosters in the city, was a true artist. She and her sister boosters would wear big bloomers under their dresses called booster drawers.

Their long overcoats or dresses hid the stolen goods. The booster would enter the store with a partner, who would distract the clerk by pretending to buy some expensive item. While the clerk was fully distracted, the booster would get busy snatching clothes off the rack and stuffing the stolen articles into the booster drawers. They'd then exit the store. Wow! How Baby Doll got away with it was beyond me. She was only five foot three and weighed a hundred and ten pounds. She'd walk in the store at her natural weight and walk out weighing a hundred and fifty-five pounds, with some of the finest dresses and suits in the store under that dress of hers. How the clerk couldn't see the difference is amazing. She was so good, you could tell her what outfit you wanted and what size you wanted it in, and Baby Doll would have it the next day. I think those shoplifting tags were invented just to save the industry from the Detroit boosters.

None of us knew Baby Doll's real name, but she was the second best booster in Detroit. Light-skinned Dorothy, who was passé Blanc and could pass for white, was number one. Neither one of them had ever been busted until then.

The captain had come to the studio to hear the new song I was working on, but instead of talking about the song, he asked me if I knew Baby Doll, the booster. I started to say no but I figured he'd done his homework, so I didn't lie.

"Yeah, I know her."

"Do you know where she is?" he asked.

That I didn't know, not at the time,

"No I don't. Why you asking? Is she in some kinda trouble?"

The captain pushed his hat back on his head, looking like a cop, and said, "We have her on camera boosting a store. We also have an eyewitness. Now I know she's a friend of yours, so if you see her, tell her she's got twenty four hours to turn herself in. You got it?"

I could tell he was serious.

"I got it," I assured him.

As the captain left the room he said, "By the way, I like the new song."

I hurried up and found Baby Doll right away and told her she had to leave town, pronto. "Don't even think about coming back to Detroit," I told her. I put her on a plane that night. I had to lend her some money, which she promised to pay back, but what the hell; I didn't care if she paid me back or not, the girl was all right with me. She saved my ass, too, later - Big time.

Watching the captain and Miss Murphy over time, it seemed to me they were in love. Nothing they did or even said that you could put your finger on exactly, but there was something in the air between them. It stayed up in the air, never coming down. I think she was married and I think he was, too. They always kept a respectable distance between themselves. And they had mutual respect for each other, for the beautiful girls who sang the music and for me. They taught me a lot about respect and loyalty and added a new word to my vocabulary. Trust! They trusted me and we became like a family. What a wonderful feeling trust is - the true foundation for love and friendship. Since trust is such a rare thing, it makes love and true friendship even rarer.

If you find all three of them, hang on, baby, 'cause you really got something. HOB records carried some other labels, including the Soul Record label, which was the R & B line. I wrote and produced records for the gospel label and the Soul line.

Miss Murphy was promoting and distributing her own labels. But her gospel label was her main focus, and it was turning out the hits and growing fast in the field of gospel music. And that was fantastic! But do you remember what I said previously about getting the blues? Well, it was back; bigger than ever this time. This gospel music thing was not working out for me. This is not what I wanted to do for the rest of my life. For a moment, yeah okay; but forever? No way! I felt like I was being boxed in and that I'd better get out of there before the lid came down on me. You see what I'm sayin.' There was a lotta love being shown to me, I'm the first to admit, and I didn't wanna seem ungrateful, but producing gospel music forever just wasn't working for me! I was making pretty good money on the side with my other hustles. I got a chance to use some of the gospel singers who could really sing, to make demos of my rhythm and blues songs. But like I said, this was not what I wanted to do. I wanted to write and produce all kind of songs, work with different kinds of artists, even do my own thing, can you feel me? Even being in heaven with all the fine girl gospel singers wore off. Now you know something was wrong with this picture; as much as I love the ladies. And I do love the ladies. Oh yeah! But don't you let the word Gospel throw you off, there was some fine sexy sista's in The House of Beauty. Be that as it may I still had to get outta there.

I had a meeting with the captain and Miss Murphy and told them what I was feeling, that I had to do my own thing. I also let them know I would produce anything for them, for no charge, whenever they needed me. We parted on a good note. Apparently, The Man Upstairs had other plans for me, too. With my debts paid off and my head cleared as well, I was in the perfect frame of mind to answer one of the most important calls of my life. It was from Berry Gordy. He was back and ready to pull his label together. He wanted to have a meeting with me at his place.

Yes! It was right on time! I was ready, man.

BERRY GORDY

When I arrived at the apartment building where Berry Gordy lived, I was a little disappointed. It was one of those ghetto fabulous security buildings, the ones with the front door buzzer that's always broken. You know the kind. You wait for someone to come out so you can grab the door just before it closes. That's what I call ghetto-fabulous.

Berry's apartment was at the very end of the hall. As I approached it, I was moving to the sound of music in my head. I could picture myself becoming a big recording star like Jackie Wilson. I saw myself singing, writing songs, producing, the whole nine yards. The excitement was mounting with every step I took. My briefcase, stuffed with all my music, suddenly felt heavy. My palms were a little sweaty. Nearing the door, I stopped and took a deep breath to calm myself down. I was getting a little too excited. Okay, Mickey, this is it! This is your big chance. I kept telling myself to stay cool! I stood there; inhaling, exhaling - inhaling, exhaling.

Before I could knock on the door, Berry opened it. His attire was what you might call understated; he stood there wearing striped boxer shorts and a T-shirt.

"Come on in and have a seat," he said. "I'm on the phone. I'll only be a minute."

When I stepped into the room, I looked around and I took in a dinky little apartment with hardly any furniture in it; a few chairs, a table and faded drapes covered the windows. For a man who's working with Jackie Wilson and writing hit songs, I thought, wow, is this guy really cheap or what?

Berry hung up the phone and started right in on me. "I heard about the work you've been doing with the local musicians and singers," he said. "I'm impressed. I also heard that you're a songwriter and producer."

"Yeah, you heard right. I sing, too."

Berry was nodding his head with approval. "That's good. Let me hear you sing some of your songs."

I started looking around again in case I'd missed it.

41

"How am I gonna sing? You ain't got no piano or nothing."

He sat down in one of the two chairs in with a half-smile, half-smirk on his face.

"You open your mouth and the words come out. That's how."

That sounded like a challenge to me so I opened my briefcase, pulled out some of my original songs, and started singing. I sang, and he listened. After about six songs, he looked at me with a blank expression on his face.

"You got any more songs?"

"Yeah I got some more," I said.

"Well! Let's hear em."

Wow! Man, I thought, he likes my songs; I can tell. This could be it: my turn as an artist doing my own thing, recording my own material. I started looking at the songs I had left. All the while I'm thinking, which one should I sing next? Which one could be my first smash hit? Man, I was excited, too excited. I was taking too long; I couldn't make up my mind.

"What's up?" Berry asked.

That's when I found it! This was the one! Yeah, this was my hit song! If Only the Sky Was a Mirror.

I decided to sing two more songs before I sang my hit song. Yeah! Place it in the best spot, the encore position. I sang the first two songs real cool and smooth. When I broke out with my hit, I sang it full throttle, with all the passion and emotion I could, showcasing the full range of my vocal style. Man, I wore it out! I was on fire. When I finished the song, I saw the look on Berry Gordy's face. No doubt, he was very impressed! I couldn't blame him, because I truly sang the hell outta that song.

"You really got some good stuff," he said, still holding his expression.

When I heard him say that, I felt great! I forgot all about his dinky little apartment. All I could see was Berry Gordy telling me that he liked my songs.

"You think I got some hit songs?"

Berry looked me straight in the eye and said, "Yeah, I think so."

"Yes! Yes!" I was so excited; I started talking fast non-stop, like I do when I'm all pumped up. "That's great. When do we get started? I mean when do I get a contract? What songs do you wanna record first? I bet it was the last one, right?! I think…"

He interrupted me in mid-sentence. "Wow, wait a minute," he said. "You got some good songs, but not with you singing them."

All the wind went outta my sails.

"It's about your voice," Berry explained. "It's not happening."

"What?" I said. "What do you mean? Are you saying you don't like my voice?"

That peculiar half-smile, half-smirk reappeared. "No, that's not what I'm saying. What I'm saying is - your voice is for shit!"

Who did this guy think he was? My voice had gotten me all over this country. My voice was for shit? I was pissed. My songs had been tossed all over his floor. I knelt down and started grabbing them and throwing them back into my briefcase as fast as I could. All I wanted to do was get the hell outta that little dinky jive-ass ghetto fabulous apartment. Berry kept talking.

"If you're gonna run the music department as the A&R man for my new record company, we've got to be honest with each other; and you gotta be honest with all the artists, writers and producers you'll be working with too."

I froze. With my songs in one hand and the briefcase half full in the other, I looked up at him. "What do you mean, A&R man? Run the department?"

Berry paused for a half second. He had my undivided attention. "Do you know what 'A&R' means?" he asked.

I looked at him. "Well, I know it has something to do with music, artists and producing."

43

Berry looked back. "Yes, that's right; Artists and Repertoire. In other words, you're gonna be responsible for putting the right artists, songwriters, producers, and musicians together to make some hit records. That's what it means. Anyway, that's what you're gonna do. Now can you handle that?"

As I stood up, I looked him straight in the eye and said, "Absolutely! I can handle that. You're telling me that I'm gonna be the A&R, whatever that is, for your company?"

"That's right," he said. "You're the man!"

The same feeling came over me that I experienced when I found a home in the Air Force. As I slowly closed my briefcase, I said, "Does that mean I'm in charge of the music, the artists, the producers, and everything?"

The smile never left his face. "That's right. You're in charge."

"I wanna know one thing," I said. "Can I record anybody I want, including myself?"
Berry shrugged his shoulders.

"I really don't want to hear you singing on anything but you're the A&R man.

Then I popped the big question. "How much do I get for running the music department as The Man?"

He explained to me how I would get royalties on every record that went out, when we had hits. That's when I would make some real money, etc. It sounded like a bunch of bullshit to me. It was not the answer I was looking for. Besides, I was already upset with this brother for what he'd said about my voice. Who did he think he was? I was ready to get out of there. Whatever I was thinking or saying to myself never fazed Berry a bit. He kept right on talking about what was going to happen for me, as the A&R man. He talked like he had no doubt in his mind that we would have some hits.

"Yeah, yeah, all that's nice," I said. "But how much money do I get paid each week? That's what I'm talking about."

Again, with the odd little smile-smirk. "We'll start you off at five dollars a day. That's twenty-five dollars a week. You're on your own on Saturdays and Sundays."

The smirk had turned into a big grin, teeth and all. In fact, he was doing everything he could to keep from laughing out loud. He just stood there grinning like he had told me a riddle and was waiting for me to shout out the answer, "Rumpelstiltskin" or something. I thought, this brother has lost his ever-lovin' mind.

I broke out laughing.

"Five dollars a day! Are you kidding me?

Berry laughed even harder.

"And all the chili you can eat; by the way, you're gonna like the chili." He started to get dressed.

I stood there, thinking. This was not turning out the way I'd thought it would. I'd come to get a record contract, not a five dollar job and a bowl of chili.

Then Berry spoke as if he could read my mind: "Don't forget, you'll be in charge."

As I finished putting the rest of my music in the briefcase, I was thinking, "This is crazy. This is nothing but chasing a dream."

Then I remembered my momma saying, "Dreams won't come true unless you start doing something about them."

A smile spread over my face. I reached out for his hand.

"When do I start?"

Berry Gordy and I shook hands, both of us laughing at the other as he said,

"Right now!

THE MAGIC OF MOTOWN– 1959

Our first building, at 2648 West Grand Boulevard in Detroit, was a two-story house, what you'd call a two-family flat.

In that building, I had my first office. It was small, but it was mine. The office was upstairs, with a desk, a piano and a roll-around chair. The chair didn't match the desk, but I could roll around from the desk to the three quarter upright piano, whose keys all worked. I just loved that!

My office must once have been the master bedroom because I had a big window that overlooked the streets. That turned out to be a good thing, because when I started auditioning, I could see who was comin' and goin'. That gave me enough time to get the hell out of there before I got trapped and had to listen to a whole-lotta terrible singers.

Berry Gordy had a plan for every room in that house, even the basement. He turned the garage into a recording studio and half of the dining room into the control room. The other half became the tape library and the front room became the reception area. Every other room became a rehearsal/writers room. All the rooms had tape recorders and pianos in them. It became clear to me that Berry Gordy, Jr., wasn't cheap; the man simply had a plan for every single dollar. Furniture, cars, apartments; none of these things were important to him. The man was on a mission, a quest, if you will.

Smokey Robinson, The Holland brothers, Lamont Dozier, and myself among others, got caught up in his charisma and enthusiasm for his quest. We all found ourselves going along without question, pursuing his dream. And soon it became our dream as well.

Thank God for dreams!

The moment you came around Motown Records, you could feel it. It was like a huge magnet drawing you closer and closer into this dream. It was beginning to turn us into a creative music machine, and we loved every minute of it.

Nothing was more exciting than the day we put the "Hitsville U.S.A." sign up on the building. We all stood outside and applauded. Then we went inside and had our usual lunch of chili and crackers.

Raynoma, Berry's wife at the time, made a mean chili. Sometimes she'd even throw in some spaghetti; now that's when it was real good! She and B.G. (that's what I started calling Berry Gordy) had formed the Rayber Music Writing Company in 1957. Back then, they would charge $100 to help with writing, arranging, making demos, whatever. We called Raynoma "Ray," for short. She was as cute as she wanted to be, and for a petite woman who couldn't have weighed more than a hundred pounds soaking wet, she had more energy than any three of us put together. She was busy all over the place. I remember how Ray would listen to the songs while we were writing them and help create some of the vocal background for songs. She would rehearse the backup singers, even sing along with them on the records if need be. Oh yeah! She could sing, too.

That was Raynoma. Ray helped create and sing background on most of singer/songwriter Marv Johnson's records. Marv had some hits, too! Songs like Come to Me, You Got What It Takes, and my favorite, I Love the Way You Love. She called her group The RayBar Voices. That's kinda cute, huh?

Marv Johnson. Let's talk about him for a moment. Marv, who was Berry Gordy's discovery, wrote hit songs with B.G. and was signed to United Artists records for a while. Marv had a couple of hits at the time, and I must admit his records helped keep us in business in the beginning. I can't take that away from him. I even conducted the orchestra for him. But it was strictly, business. Everybody catered to Marv, everybody but me. I never catered to anybody. He never really liked me, which was okay because I wasn't crazy about him either. You see, Brother Marv Johnson thought he was the shit, a Black superstar. I thought he was just lucky enough to have Berry Gordy and the Motown machine behind him.

He was the only thing we had going at the time, so his ego was bigger than his ass, which I had to straighten out a couple of times. The brother was always late for his recording sessions. Marv would ride around in his big black Caddy with his silk suits on, smoking weed and talkin' shit to the girls - knowing he was holding up my producers, musicians and me in the studio. Some artists could get that way with one or two hits, but in this company, I was in charge of the music, the studio, and the artists, and I wasn't taking no mess off of nobody; and that included Mister Marv Johnson.

AUDITIONS

Nobody was happier than I was when we got our first hit records on our label; Please Mr. Postman by the Marvelettes and Shop Around by the Miracles.

When those records took off, I had no concept of what was about to happen, but I soon found out. It seemed like the floodgates opened and people started pouring in. It was during the auditions that I got a chance to learn a lot more about what an A&R man's responsibilities were, and what they meant to the lifeline of a record company.

The auditions were the hardest part of the job, both challenging and frightening. Making the decision to reject someone's writing or singing was very difficult for me. Not knowing or understanding the desperate state of mind some of the people were in did not help. You gotta understand this was all new to me and I didn't yet have the temperament, patience, or even the knowledge for handling the countless numbers of talented and non-talented people who bombarded us at Hitsville U.S.A.

When word got out that I was looking for singers, writers, producers, and musicians, the people came nonstop. It didn't matter about the date or the time set for auditions, they came whenever they wanted to. All the things I learned and the training I got on the road wasn't half enough to prepare me for the onslaught of artists that bombarded Motown, the only music outlet for Black talent that was on fire.

There had been other independent record companies; Atlantic, Arista, Chess, Vee-Jay Records, King, A&M, Casablanca, as well as up-and-comers like Stax, Philly International and Solar, to name a few. But none of them were ever on fire like Motown! Ours was a house built on a solid foundation of love and devotion to talented Black artists with a commitment to win. Somehow that message reached young people all over America, and they came to audition for Motown. If they thought they could sing they came, if they wished they could sing they came.

They came as writers, musicians, producers, even the dreamers came, wanting to be a part of The Motown Sound of Young America. The majority of them had no possibilities whatsoever; nevertheless, they came from all over Michigan, Ohio, Illinois, even as far away as New York and California.

The Motown fever had caught on and everybody wanted to be part of it. I had auditions going on every day. I couldn't just turn the people away; I didn't have the heart. Like I said, I wasn't ready for this audition business, my God! There were so many. I handled it the only way I knew how. I made it up as I went along.

Some of my auditions went like this - When an artist walked into my office, I would immediately ask him, What is it that you do? Sing or write? If they said they were a writer, I'd say, Show me your stuff. If it was bad (and most of it was terrible!), I would say; what the hell was that? That's not a song! Come back when you got some experience. Next!

If they said they were a singer, I'd say; Start singing right now! If they hesitated for a second, I would immediately put them out of my office and tell them to come back when they could sing on the spot. Next!

You see what I mean? I had no tact or diplomacy, none whatsoever. I had no idea how sensitive some of those people were. All I knew was they were terrible and they didn't have a clue. There was always a line of people waiting to audition, and there was no way to judge a book by its cover, so I had to give everybody a chance. Every time I got sick and tired of seeing so many bad artists, and got ready to call it a day, someone would come in and blow me away. That made a whole week of disastrous auditions worth it.

Some came in as singers and found they were better writers, some came in as writers and found out they were better singers, and so on. The biggest problem they had in getting through my unusual auditioning process was; no matter how good you were in the audition, you still had to convince me that if I signed you to Motown, you would not get sidetracked by anything or anybody. You would stay focused on your career and work hard at being the best you could be. If you could show me that, you had a chance.

Steve Lever, who was an agent with the William Morris Talent and Literary Agency, is said to have remarked that "Motown was the original American Idol. Randy Jackson, Paula Abdul, and Simon Cowell, all three of them were rolled up into one person; William Mickey Stevenson, the A&R man at Motown."

We were a Black-owned company powered by a feeling of unity and pride. The whole Motown phenomenon happened at a time in America when Black pride and unity were badly needed. Leaders like Adam Clayton Powell, the Reverend Martin Luther King, the Reverend Al Sharpton, the

Reverend Jesse Jackson, Malcolm X and others, in their own way, were all pushing Black pride and unity. Even James Brown jumped in with his hit song, I'm Black and I'm Proud. Motown, in its own way, was showing people in the industry, artists, and in general, that unity among Black people was not only a possibility; it was a reality.

The fans, who were multiplying by the thousands, took pride in seeing Motown grow. Talented people all over the country believed that if they could get with Motown, they had a fighting chance of making it, and they were right. Not to mention the fact that we were putting out some great records. We were firmly committed to every new artist that I signed to Motown. We were out to develop them to their greatest potential.

I remember when the Velvelettes (He Was Really Sayin' Somethin') showed up to audition. It was on a Saturday and they had driven all the way down from Kalamazoo, Michigan. They had convinced their father, a minister, to let them audition for Motown. When they arrived, they were told by the receptionist that the auditions were over, and they had to make an appointment on Monday. The girls were just crushed! They didn't know how they were going to explain this to their father.

Just as they were leaving the building, I happened to come down the stairs from my office. I was on my way to the studio for a session when one of the Velvelettes noticed me. She remembered working for me as a background singer. She immediately called out my name, real loud. "Mr. Stevenson, Mr. Mickey Stevenson!"

She got my attention and started running down her sob story about coming all the way from Kalamazoo, and how they didn't know about the audition time on Saturday, and their father being a minister and letting them come, the whole tearjerker. She was talking faster than a machine gun on St. Valentine's Day.

Now I had auditioned so many terrible artists in the prior two weeks that I really wasn't in the mood for another one. Besides, I was in a hurry to get back into the studio. While I was thinking how to get rid of her nicely, she was still talking. The only way I was gonna make it to the studio was to shut her up. She was quite convincing, pushy, and confident, qualities that I had learned to admire in this business, so I told her, "You got five minutes to get the rest of your girls in here and let me hear what you got. Let's do it! Right here in the lobby. Go!"

She ran out to the car and brought the girls back. They sang two songs

51

for me, I signed them up quick fast and in a hurry, and the rest is history. The most persistent artist to audition was Martha Reeves; this was before the Vandellas. Martha hounded me until I had to listen to her, and that was after I ducked and dodged her for weeks. After hearing her sing, I still didn't sign her. It's not that she wasn't good, I was just up to my ears with female singers.

They were all driving me up a wall with their boyfriend problems, parent problems, petty jealousies, you name it, they had it goin' on. Being the A&R man was tough enough, and I loved it, but I also had to be a father, a therapist, a brother, even a best friend and mentor to some of the artists.

Emotional tussles went on throughout the day, and it was nothing for me to get a distress call from an artist in the middle of the night. I would have to get outta my comfortable position, with whomever, and try to resolve the problem.

MARTHA REEVES

I was in my office on the phone when Martha walked in. She wheedled her way back into the building, again, to try and convince me to sign her - again. By now she had become a familiar face around the Motown buildings and was able to work her way into my office. Before I could give her a piece of my mind, for the umpteenth time, I was called to the president's office for a meeting. When I returned, Martha was on my phone taking messages.

I couldn't believe it. I stood there waiting for her to get off my phone so I could really tell her a thing or two. While watching and listening to her talk on the phone, I realized that she was good at it. In fact, she was really good at it. When she saw the expression on my face she handed me about ten messages she had taken, and kept on talking. I looked them over and, to my surprise they were complete with all the proper information. She had the "who, what, when," and all that good stuff covered.

I was impressed. I handed her one of the messages, "Get this person back on the line."

She called the party back. "Just one moment please; Yes, Mr. Stevenson would like to speak with you."

When she handed me the phone, she had a look on her face and an attitude that said, I know how to do this.

I finished the call and said, "Martha, obviously you're gonna hang around here until you drive me crazy or get a record deal out of me, so here's what I'm gonna do. I'm putting you on as my secretary."

"Could you make that an assistant?" she asked.

"Don't push it, Martha. Okay, assistant it is; but on a trial basis, mind you. We'll talk about a recording contract later."

Her smile lit up the room. Martha didn't ask about money or anything, she just started organizing the desk and answering the phones. She had said she could handle it and she could indeed handle it; she managed the phones, the artists and the musicians without going crazy. It took a lot of self-control to handle one musician in particular, our drummer Benny

Benjamin. My man Benny could drive you up a wall about some money. We'll get to him later.

Martha kept my sessions in good order as well. Above all, she knew how to keep people off my back. Whenever I worked late--and that was all the time - Martha would stay as late as I would. She would hang in there without being asked to stay. Martha loved to be around Motown as much as the rest of us did.

Months later, I ordered some contracts for Gino Parks and André Williams, you remember them? They were the two guys who sang at Denny's Show Bar, the night club, below my old apartment. When Martha put their contracts on my desk for my signature, I noticed another contract. It was hers.

"What is this, Martha?"

"Oh, that's my contract! Now, Mickey Stevenson, you may as well sign it. I didn't forget and I ain't going anywhere. If you want me to stop bugging you about this contract and start asking you for overtime pay..."

I immediately put my hand up, signaling her to shut up.

"Martha," I said, "that sounds like blackmail to me." I looked at her and smiled. I knew she was right about the overtime, and I sure didn't wanna hear her running her mouth every single day asking me about some damn contract. I knew she wasn't going anywhere, so I signed it... to shut her up.

I had no intention of doing any recording with her any time soon. Martha was a damn good secretary (Oh! I'm sorry; I mean assistant) and I didn't want to lose her. I'm selfish? Maybe, but that's the way it was. Little did I know - Martha would record one of the biggest singles in Motown history.

It all started when Marvin Gaye, songwriter/producer Ivy Jo Hunter and I just finished recording the track to a song we had written. We were working on it for Kim Weston. You see, I had promised Kim a hit, and we felt this was it, only we had a problem. Kim was a great ballad singer with a deep, rich voice, but that was not the sound we heard on this song. We had to find a way to get her to approach this song differently, the way we heard it when we wrote it. I had my work cut out for me. It was very late that evening when we finished tracking the song.

Martha was there, like always, and that's when I came up with this great idea. I would let Martha overdub the song the way we wanted it to sound, and this would give us a vocal demo for Kim to study. The beauty of this idea was, I would be giving Martha some attention in the studio and that would keep her from bugging me about recording her. I'd kill two birds with one stone .You see what I'm saying? Buying time I called it, how sweet it is! I loved it!

I took Martha into the control room and gave her the lyrics to look over. We gave her some idea of how we wanted her to sing the song. When she was ready, she went into the studio, got on the mic and went to work recording it. Now when Martha finished singing that song, a complete silence fell over the control room. Marvin Gaye, Ivy Jo and I all looked at each other, in shock! We all heard and felt the same thing.

Martha sung that song like a star. She'd done it just the way we wanted to hear it. The conclusion was unanimous: Dancing in the Street would be a hit for Martha Reeves. Ivy Jo, who had vowed not to comb his hair until he had a number one record, started rubbing his nappy head. "William R.," he said, using the producers' nickname for me, "I think we got one, bro, a worldwide number one!"

All of a sudden, I was faced with a huge problem, much bigger than the one I'd started with. Never count your chickens before they hatch, you see what I'm saying? We all knew there was no way Kim Weston was gonna sing that song the way Martha Reeves just had. No way!

Hang on, it gets worse.

Here I am, the A&R man with the reputation and the responsibility for putting the right artists on the right songs, William R. Stevenson, "the man" known for delivering the hits, showing no favoritism, taking no prisoners, putting the company first and all that jazz. But to add insult to injury, Kim Weston was my woman at the time.

Now try that on for size. I was caught between a rock and a hard place.

Marvin looked at me and broke out laughing. "I wouldn't wanna be in your shoes right now, William R., not for nothing in the world."

Ivy Jo, with his smart ass, chimed in. "Hey bro, you are the A&R man 'round here, right? So you already got the shoes on your feet! And we got us a hit record in the can."

He started to scratch his nappy head again and got all excited. "This song could go to number one, bro, all over the world! So whatcha gonna do? You're the man!"

I said the only thing I could think to say. "I'm gonna try Kim on the song and see if she can cut it. That's what I'm gonna' do!"

Ivy Jo laughed so hard he could hardly speak. "Did I hear you say, give Kim a try? Ha ha ha! Try what? I know you're not talking about her singing that song. William R., you know better than anybody in this building that would be a waste of time."

He was really beginning to piss me off, but the brother was right. I would be wasting my time. There was no way Kim was gonna get that song, no way!

Marvin shook his head as he walked out of the control room. "I know you, William R. Martha is gonna have a hit, and you are gonna lose your woman."

"Marvin, I don't believe that would happen over a song, man!" I shot back. "And another thing, what kinda love is that?"

Marvin turned to me and said, "That's not just a song, it's a hit song! And Kim is not just your woman, she is a recording artist. But you already know all that. Like I said, William R., I'd hate to be in your shoes."

Ivy Jo just couldn't resist jumping in. "You can always get another woman, bro, but how many number one worldwide hit records like this are we gonna get?"

He got carried away with laughter again.

"Ha, ha, ha! I was just kidding about the woman part, bro."

He wasn't kidding. He meant every damn word he said. That was the first time I wanted to just slap him upside his woolly head.

When I got to Kim's apartment, it was about three in the morning. I stopped at the after-hours joint and had a couple of drinks. I had to figure out just how I was going to approach this thing with Kim. I tried to convince myself that she would understand this was my job, it's what I do.

I leaned on the doorbell for a long time. Kim was a hard sleeper, but I finally woke her up. When she came to the door, I gave her a big hug, telling her about the song we'd written and that I wanted her to hear it right then.

"What time is it, baby?" she said, looking at the clock. "Baby, it's almost four in the morning. I'm too sleepy to…"

Before she could finish the sentence, I had the song playing on the box. I had the volume down low. She was half asleep, listening; nodding in and out. I played it for her over and over again. After listening to it four or five times Kim turned to me and said,

"I'll sing it baby, but I don't really like it. Now baby, you coming to bed?"

I turned the record off and calmly told her, "Hey baby, if you don't like it, you don't have to sing it. I'll find you something else. Go on back to sleep."

When I walked into the studio the next day, Ivy Jo and Marvin were waiting for me. Of course, Mister Smart Mouth Ivy Jo couldn't wait. "Well, what happened, bro? Is Kim locking you out or what?"

I looked at them nonchalantly. "Nothing happened," I said. "I did my job like I always do. Martha is doing the song."

Marvin gave me a hard high five. "You the man, William R.! You are the man!"

I turned to Ivy Jo, looked him in the eyes and said, "And you go get a haircut bro!"

After Kim got wind of the smash hit song, "Dancing in the Street," and that it was coming out with Martha and the Vandellas, all hell broke loose. She was pissed off. She hardly spoke to me for weeks. Sadly, sex was out altogether. I finally came up with an idea to remedy the situation. You're gonna love this.

I talked Kim into cooking a big meal for the producers, Holland-Dozier-Holland (Lamont Dozier and brothers; Brian and Eddie Holland).

Kim Weston could cook like her momma, who weighed over three hundred pounds from good cookin' and good eatin'. I knew that H.D.H. hadn't eaten like this in years; I'm talking about real Southern fried chicken, smothered pork chops with mac and cheese, candied yams, collard greens, and peach cobbler.

H.D.H. walked into the house and the aroma from all that good food hit 'em like a hit record. Lamont Dozier called out, "Kim Weston, where is the food, girl?"

"Just follow your nose," she said.

The boys started eating and didn't stop. In the middle of Eddie Holland's third helping, he asked Kim, "What can we do for you?"

I jumped in. "She needs a hit record."

Brian Holland, now reaching for his third helping, said, "You got it!"

They didn't stop eating until most of the food was gone. What they didn't eat they took back to the studio and came up with a hit song for Kim; Take Me in Your Arms (Rock Me a Little While).

Dancing in the Street was released by Martha and the Vandellas, and when it went to number one, Ivy Joe got his hair cut and Marvin Gaye bought a motorcycle.

And the hits just kept coming.

HOW NOT TO HANDLE AUDITIONS

It was one of those cold winter days in Detroit, and the huge falling snowflakes were painting a beautiful picture. Larry Maxwell, the promotion man, was standing with me outside the building, having a smoke and admiring the view. As we started to go back inside, out of nowhere we heard gunshots. Bang! Bang!

I looked down the street and saw a man running toward us with a gun in his hand. His overcoat was unbuttoned and flying in the air. He looked like Batman running with a pistol between his legs and a pistol in his hand. Except for his coat, the man was naked, to the bone and screaming like a maniac. "You ruined my career, you ruined my career!"

When he fired the gun again, Maxwell ran inside shouting, "Mickey, he's shooting at you!" I took another look and realized he was shooting at me! By the time a cop got Batman under control and put him in the police car, I got a good look at the shooter and I recognized him. He had auditioned for me.

I remembered his audition because he was terrible and his song was terrible. It was so bad, I told him not to quit his day job. Not only would he go hungry as a singer, I told him, he'd starve to death as a writer. He told me how all of his friends thought his song was great, his voice was great and I didn't know what I was talking about. I had to put the brother out of my office.

Well, I don't have to tell you I learned how not to handle an audition. From that day on, I had a set spiel for all the rejects; especially the terrible ones because they're the most passionate and the most explosive. My spiel went like this; "Your voice is something else. It's different, and your song is nice, but I gotta tell you at this time, Motown is not quite ready for an artist like you. But if you come back in about six to eight months, I think we might be ready for an artist of your caliber."

That was my rap, and I stuck with it.

THE FUNK BROTHERS

The Motown music machine was growing fast, and my department was growing with it. I was signing more artists, producers, and writers. Adjustments had to be made; some of the new writers and producers I assigned to the new artists. And some of the better writers I teamed up with the veteran producers, so they could sharpen their skills against each other.

Some worked out and some didn't. Manipulating and adjusting writers and producers, hoping you that you will come up with the best results, was a nonstop effort and commitment on all of our parts. I tried some of everything; you name it, I did it.

Sometimes a writer would come up with a strong hook or phrase, even a hot rhythm that was catchy and unique, but he might not have a story, or the melody would be weak.

As the A&R man, I would team this writer up with another writer who could add a lyric, a melody or maybe a stronger story, to the hook, phrase or rhythm. Sometimes the match would be an instant success! And sometimes it would almost be there but not quite. Something would still be missing. That's when I would add or suggest a third creative person to join the team, and guess what?

The Magic would happen. Yes!

A whole flock of Motown songs would have two or three writers on one song. Check it out. The same process worked with producers. What made it so wonderful, working and creating at Motown, was that to make a hit song, almost everyone would welcome help from another creative person. To get these creative people together and into a mindset to cooperate with each other, I would give everyone my Songwriters and Producers Speech. It went like this;

"If the song you're working on is the only song you're ever going to write or produce, then don't share it with anyone. Keep that good stuff to yourself. But if you want to grow as a songwriter, a producer, or both, it behooves you to think about this. It's a wonderful thing to work and create with others. You will learn from each other. Consequently, you will write and create more songs, better songs, even hit songs."

That was my speech and I stand by it to this day.

There were, of course, writers and producers who didn't listen. I had to let them go. I had to cut those who couldn't cut it. You can't make adjustments like that without creating enemies, and brother, I had my hands full of 'em. They would go to B.G. (that's what everybody started calling The Chairman) complaining about how I mistreated them. B.G. would listen to their complaints with empathy and then he would tell them they'd have to work it out with the A&R man. "That's his department."

From the day the chairman and I shook hands in his apartment, and he dubbed me The Man, he meant it. I was The Man! He seldom interfered with any decisions I made within my department, good, bad, or otherwise. When I made great decisions, I got praises and raises. When I made bad decisions, I paid for them big time! The money came out of my budget, my pocket, or both! B.G. didn't play around.

I liked calling the chairman B.G. and I call him that to this day. I was known as William R. to some and Mickey to others, but the musicians had another name for me. They called me Il Duce. "Il Duce" was Benito Mussolini's handle. I was given that name by the drummer Benny Benjamin. (I mentioned him earlier, remember?)

Part of the magic of Motown was the creative sound of the rhythm section, of which Benny Benjamin was a staple. He was part of the legendary Funk Brothers.

Let's talk about the gathering of The Funk Brothers.

Searching for the best of the best sounds for Motown, I spent many nights going in and out of every nightclub, bar, and joint that had live music in it. I was looking for the most talented and the hungriest musicians I could find. Being talented was great, but to go along with us, a musician had to be hungry as well. That was as important as being talented.

Finally, I found the ones I wanted. I told them that if they joined us now and became part of the Motown family, it would pay off big time. Everybody had to understand that we were a growing company, and they would have to grow with us. I leveled with them that the money wasn't long, but the sessions were plenty. As we grew, so would the money. "You got my word on that," I'd promise.

Some of the musicians I eventually found knew me and had worked for me before. They knew my word was good, and they agreed to go along for the ride. I stuck to my word, and they became one of the greatest rhythm sections in the business, a family within a family. We called them The Funk Brothers. I love' em all! The wonderful pulsating sound of The Funk Brothers was the heartbeat of The Motown Music Machine.

Standing in the Shadows of Motown was a nice movie about The Funk Brothers. The movie had some good moments in it, and I enjoyed it even though neither Berry Gordy, Smokey Robinson nor William Mickey Stevenson aka "Il Duce" were portrayed in the movie. Now I'm not upset about not being in the movie myself, even though I put The Funk Brothers together. I'm really not upset, okay! Let me tell you why. Most of the original Funk Brothers were not in the movie either; I'm talking about Benny Benjamin, James Jamerson, Earl "The Fingers" Van Dyke, Bongo Eddie Brown, or Robert White. None of them were in "Standing in the Shadows of Motown."

Now when you add the names of Eddie Willis, Joe Hunter, Joe Messina and Jack Ashford to the missing four, you have the original Funk Brothers. And like I said, I loved all of them. Did you get it? Are you sure? Well, let me help those of you who might have missed it. Let's spend a little more time on this amazing group of gifted musicians. The Funk Brothers, the anchor of the Motown sound.

The recording studio was called The Snake Pit, a name I never liked. It reminded me of that movie with the same name, with Olivia de Havilland, who spends most of the movie in an insane asylum. There was nothing crazy about the people working in our studio; at least not the same kinda crazy. We were insane over music and artists recording sessions in the studio around the clock, 24-7! Maybe that's what they were referring to when they said "snake pit."

I still didn't like the name.

THE DRUMMER

I had back up musicians for every player, including the drummer. Let me rephrase that. I should say especially the drummer! When I couldn't find Papa Zita - that was Benny Benjamin's nickname - I had two backups for that brother. Richard "Pistol" Allen and Uriel Jones were both very good drummers. And by the way, Benny named himself Papa Zita. Now you know he was out there. But he was Amazing! I loved him even though he was a pain in the butt!

Benny Benjamin was an extraordinary drummer. He was the only addict I knew of who never missed a beat. High, drunk or sober, he was a human metronome. Some of the producers would not, and I mean would not, record without him. That meant two or three times a week, I had to hold up the session, get in my car with a couple of the boys to ride shotgun, and check his favorite after-hours joints and dope houses until I found him. After doing this search thing for a while, I had it down to a science. I'd find him every single time, drag him out of the place kicking and screaming, get him to the studio, prop him up on the drums, and turn him loose.

The man was phenomenal. He'd play session after session, and when he stopped playing, he would try to get out of the studio by telling me one of his ridiculous lies.

"Hey, Il Duce," he'd say, "I got to go home for a minute, man! I forgot to feed my dogs. They haven't eaten in three or four days, man. They got to be hungry as hell by now, probably starving to death or dead maybe. Let me have about fifty dollars, Il Duce. You know I'm good for it. You can take it outta my session money. I'll be right back, I swear."

"Benny, my man, you're talking to me, remember?" I'd say. "You don't have a dog. You don't even like dogs, remember? Now how about you take your ass back in that studio and finish the sessions, please."

Benny would look at me, roll his eyes, and go back to the drums. An hour later, he'd be back with another story about his sister or his mother. I wouldn't say a word. I'd just stand there and look at him. He would get the message, roll his eyes and go back to the drums. I'd stand in the control room where everyone could see me, to make sure Benny, or anyone else for that matter, wouldn't leave.

I had sessions to finish, and nobody was getting out of there until it was over. That's why the musicians called me Il Duce.

Not only was Benny Benjamin an essential part of The Funk Brothers, he was in my opinion one of the greatest drummers in the world. He died in 1969. Benny played on his first hit in 1960, Money That's What I Want.

Within nine years he had helped create a sound that has lasted over fifty years and is still going strong. My brother Benny finally made the Rock and Roll Hall of Fame in 2003.

Better late than never, I always say.

THE BASS PLAYER

I knew about James Jamerson before I took the job as A&R man. I would see him in the clubs around the city. He'd be playing his upright bass with his eyes closed, his head bobbin' and his mouth making the sound of the notes as he played them on the bass, like the funky jazz musicians do when they're locked into a groove. James played from the heart always. When I didn't like what the other players were playing, I could follow the hot creative lick on his upright bass and still enjoy the song.

The brother was good! Jamerson knew how to take you on a musical ride with him. Yes indeed! I was a James Jamerson fan.

I used to watch him offstage waiting for the next set, drinking alone and thinking. He always looked like he was pondering something, real deep in thought. Sometimes we would have a drink or two together, but I never asked him what the problem was and he never volunteered the information. Brother Jamerson had a complex personality and he was also very emotional. Even in the conversations we had, he could easily get emotionally charged up while expressing his point of view. You know what I mean?

Jamerson knew he was a good musician, but he never got his props. I'm talking about his fair share of recognition. At that time I was in the business of helping musicians collect their money. Helping them get respect and acknowledgment was not my thing. So we would just talk about music. This way he could stay cool and I could learn something. But just between me and you, I assumed the brother's problems were not only about the money, although he could have used some more money.

When I became the A&R man for Motown, Jamerson was one of the first musicians I went after. I gave him a weekly guarantee with more to come. He got some respect from me for his talent and got paid for it, too. The brother was absolutely committed and hard to stop. I gotta tell you, this emotionally complex thing he had, was totally under control the day he became part of the Motown family. That made life easier for him and everyone else on the sessions, and that included the producer, the artist, and the rest of the soon-to-be Funk Brothers. They all had their own opinions about the music, and how it should be played. Should it be like this, or like that?

Jamerson's response would be "Hey! Let's stop talking about it, let's just get it on and see where it takes us. Somebody kick it off!"

The drummer would call it; "1-2, 1-2-3-4," and James Jamerson would let his fender bass do the talking for him.

The fender bass spoke loud and clear. The other players would feel it and, one by one, fall in the pocket, baby. It was on.

Now you see why I picked Jamerson to be the anchor for The Funk Brothers. From 1959 until I resigned from Motown, Jamerson and I never had a misunderstanding. I understood him and he understood me. I take great pride in saying we made great music throughout our years at Motown.

Motown Records moved its operation to Los Angeles in 1972 to get closer to the movie business. By this time I had resigned from Motown and was living in L. A. Jamerson thought he'd try the west coast as well. Out of nowhere I got a call from him - he wanted to talk. I was very happy to hear from him. We had lunch that very afternoon. I gotta tell you I was all set for this great session with an old friend.

We started with a few drinks and talked about Motown, the artists, the sessions, The Funk Brothers, you name it. After a few more drinks, and I mean quite a few, the laughter got thinner. A look slipped onto Jamerson's face that I hadn't seen in years, but for some reason I recognized it. I remembered seeing it back in the day, when I was a fan of his; listening to him play the upright bass in the clubs. It was a strange look, like he was trying to figure it all out. It was a look I had never questioned before, only this time I decided to take a chance.

"What is it?" I asked.

He explained that he had never received the credit or even the recognition for all the hits he played on, for all the millions of records he knew he helped sell.

"William R.," he said, "they didn't even mention my name until last year, man. They waited all this time as if I didn't even exist until last year, man."

I began to feel his pain. As he poured out his feelings, the look on his face made me feel very uncomfortable; even worse, somehow I began to feel I had let him and the other musicians down.

I told him that I kinda felt responsible for everything. I even apologized.

"What are you apologizing for, William R.?" he asked.

"I was the A&R man, in charge of all the musicians, that's what for and I…"

Before I could finish, Jamerson hit the table with his hand and became emotional.

"I'm not talking about being in charge, man. I'm talking about the feeling you get when you see your name on some hit records and everybody knows who you are. You know what I mean man? Come on man, you know that feeling. I can see it in your face. I played my ass off, man, and they didn't know me. That's what I'm talkin' about."

He took another drink and just sat there staring into space. I waited for a moment and then I broke the silence.

"I gotta tell you, man, when you put it like that, brother, I really know I should have done something! I just didn't know any better, I was too busy doing my A&R thing. I didn't have the knowledge or the foresight to look this far ahead. Hell! If I'd had that kinda wisdom or foresight I would have been promoting myself as well, preparing for my own life after Motown. Like I said, man, I was learning what to do, and frankly, James, I'm still learning."

I found myself getting very emotional and for the next few moments we both just sat there, real quiet like; Jamerson with his head down, and me just staring into space thinking about what I could have done, if anything. Neither one of us had enough to drink to be drunk, but we'd had enough to know there was really nothing left to say.

He looked at me and very softly said, "I'm not blaming you, William R., or anybody else. I just had to get it off my chest, man."

Jamerson had that same disturbing look on his face as he got up from the table. Reaching over to shake my hand, he said, "I could always talk to you, William R. See you later." Then he walked away.

I sat there for a little while, feeling very heavy in my heart and mentally very guilty.

James Jamerson died in 1983 and in 2000 he made The Rock And Roll Hall of Fame.

The Hall of Fame is one of the highest forms of recognition for his tremendous contribution to music, to Motown and to me. I felt a little relief, but I wish we could have done more while he was alive.

Later, in 2000, James Jamerson and The Funk Brothers received the Grammy Lifetime Achievement Award.

Once again, I say better late than never.

THE PIANO PLAYER

The piano player, organ player and leader of The Funk Brothers we called Fingers. Earl Van Dyke's fingers were big and thick, and his hands seem to have a mind of their own. When his fingers touched the keyboard it was like freedom to Earl. You could see it in his eyes and in his attitude.

It was 1962 when James Jamerson showed up at the studio with Earl Van Dyke. Earl had just come off some tour that apparently was cut short. He needed another gig quick fast and in a hurry; the brother could use some money. He talked with Jamerson, who convinced him to come to Detroit and see his man William R. the A&R man at Motown.

Meanwhile, Jamerson was in the studio pumping me up about this fantastic piano player I needed to meet. James was promising me that I would not be disappointed, that brother Earl Van Dyke was the bomb (that means great) and that Earl would work with me financially, that it would not be a problem. The day Earl walked into Hitsville, the timing couldn't have been better. I had a session about to start, so while Jamerson was introducing me to Earl and telling me how great he was, I was busy walking the brother right into the studio. I gave him the chords sheet to the session, talked it over with the musicians and kicked off the tempo;

"1-2, 1-2-3-4."

We went right into the song, hot and heavy. With Benny on drums, Jamerson on bass, Robert White, Joe Messina and Eddie Willis all on guitar, and Bongo Eddie Brown on congas, it was on. I couldn't believe it! You could feel the funk, you could touch the funk, and you could even smell the funk, wow!

Baby, the chemistry was working. It was so tight and hot that when the song was over, the musicians could not stop jammin'. They had hit a groove (that's when the players stay on the same chords) that was a hypnotic chunk of funk; it went on for five minutes. We could make whole other song out of it.

When they finally stopped playing, everybody gave Earl Van Dyke the high five and he gave all of them praise. I called Earl out of the studio to cut him a deal. I offered him $150 a week guaranteed and more to come. I told him I already had two piano players, Joe Hunter and Johnny Griffin, who was with us from the beginning, "but I gotta tell you, Earl, you really got something that I need, so as of right now, if you want the deal, you're on."

Earl accepted the deal and became part of the Motown family.

This was the beginning of The Original Funk Brothers. About six weeks later, Joe Hunter, who was the main piano player, left the studio for a while. Frankly, I think it was because all the producers, including me, fell in love with Earl Van Dyke.

I immediately made Earl the bandleader for The Funk Brothers before Brother Joe Hunter changed his mind and wanted back in. And the rest of Earl Van Dyke's history is written in the Motown books of musical history.

Stay with me now, I got two more to go.

THE PERCUSSIONIST

Bongo Eddie Brown! Now this brother was a real piece of work. Bongo Eddie could play every kind of rhythm on a drum you could think of. And he had the drums to play everything on, too. Latin, Cuban, African, Indian, whatever, he could mix them all up at the same time if he wanted to. The brother was as good as they get.

Bongo Eddie joined our family around the same time Earl Van Dyke came aboard. Eddie was not into material things, not at all. He would wear his caps, his vest and his tennis shoes everywhere. The brother lived in the basement of an apartment building. It was just a wide open space with a bathroom and some furniture that consisted of a bed, a hot plate, a miniature refrigerator, and a clothes rack that came right out of some theater's dressing room.

The brother had a collection of exotic drums and percussion instruments of all shapes and sizes, showcased in an art deco arrangement. The moment you saw his magnificent collection of drums, you knew exactly where all his money went. I must admit it was very interesting to look at his collection of drums and things, especially after you smoked some of his heavy duty grass. And this brother always had some of the best marijuana I ever had. Smoking his grass was one of the reasons Bongo Eddie was oblivious to the rest of the world. His world would come alive jammin' with The Funk Brothers, Oh yeah! And a hot chick every now and then! He was in total heaven every time he played his bongo drums. On a session, at a gig, or in the club, it didn't matter. Playing with The Funk Brothers was his life. In the studio, he would release all of his emotions; joy, love and anger, even his frustration about the unfair treatment that his Black brothers and sisters had to endure. Oh yeah! "Prejudice is racism at its worst," he would say. The brother was deep. As soon as he got high off some of that fantastic marijuana of his, he could talk for hours, or as long as the grass held out.

Like I said, Bongo Eddie Brown was a piece of work. I could write ten pages on him, but they would all end up saying the same thing - Bongo Eddie's life was playing his drums and percussion instruments with The Funk Brothers. He could get off with The Funk Brothers, he was a Funk Brother, and he went on to a better world in '92, still a Funk Brother. You feel me!

THE TAMBOURINE MAN

Jack Ashford was the last addition to the Original Funk Brothers. Brother Jack, whom I called Mr. Tambourine Man, stood over six feet tall. He was lean, with long arms and a smile on his face at all times. He could play the hell out of the vibraphone. His vibe playing was very rhythmic. He was a jazz musician and Jack knew his stuff. What we didn't know was how good he was on the tambourine.

It was during one of our hot sessions that Jack was asked to play the tambourine, to add a different effect to the rhythm. When Jack picked up the tambourine and joined Bongo Eddie on the congas and Benny Benjamin on the drums, they entered a whole new world of rhythm; Jack established a spiritual touch to the Motown sound that could not be denied. It was laid back but definitely present. When the tambourine was not there you missed it, and when it was there you felt it. It worked so well and Jack was so good that playing the tambourine became his main calling with the producers.

The Funk Brothers gained another brother. He still plays the hell out the vibraphone. Hey Jack! If you're reading this, I thought I'd let the readers know about your spiritual side.

When you add the guitar players, Eddie Willis, Joe Messina and Robert White, and Joe Hunter, you have The Original Funk Brothers. The Funk Brothers grew and other great players were added; Johnny Griffith, Bob Babbitt, Uriel Jones and Richard "Pistol" Allen.

Grammy Award-winning Hall of Famers, The Funk Brothers are said to have played on more number one records than The Beatles, The Beach Boys, The Rolling Stones and Elvis Presley combined. They received their star on the Hollywood Walk of Fame March 21, 2013. It was a day to remember!

Stevie Wonder opened his speech by saying, "When I came to Motown, the first person I met was the A&R Man, William Mickey Stevenson." He concluded with a plea that everyone should do their part in keeping music in our schools.

After Stevie, they called up trombonist Paul Riser, who talked about meeting Motown's A&R man, Mickey Stevenson, right after he graduated

The A&R Man / William Mickey Stevenson

from Detroit's prestigious Cass Technical High in 1962.

"Mickey didn't waste any time with me," he told the crowd. "After hearing me blow my horn, he laid it on me. He told me I had a lot of talent, but there's a difference between blowing notes according to theory and feeling the notes according to reality. He told me what I needed was a soulful experience. Without hesitation," Riser said, "Mickey dropped me in The Snake Pit with the other horn players."

Paul Riser began his career at Motown as a session trombonist in the pit. There he had the opportunity to work with The Funk Brothers, who helped him develop his skills. Paul eventually was propelled to the top as one of Motown's premier arrangers.

There is no way I could talk about the musicians at Motown without saluting all the brothers who were down in the Snake Pit making hits with the rest of us. "Beans" Boles, Hank Cosby, Paul Riser, and others, personally I consider them all Funk Brothers and part of the Motown family.

Now let's set the record straight. I found them, I put them together, and I named them! The Funk Brothers.

And the hits just kept on coming.

76

IL DUCE

Like I said, the Funk Brothers called me "Il Duce." Some of the women of Motown had much nicer names for me, names that made Il Duce, sound like baby love. They called me a chauvinist pig or that asshole, and a few other choice words that even I'm too proud to mention, okay. And to think young ladies were calling me names like that!

They called me all those undignified names because I wouldn't allow them to produce any artists. And if they were the artists, and had studio time tied up, they were well advised not to bring me any female problems as an excuse for being late or not showing up at all.

Above all, it was forbidden to come to the recording session not knowing the lyrics to the songs. You can't put your heart into a song while you're reading it off some paper you've had for a week or more. Whenever I'd see an artist reading the lyrics in a recording session, I'd stop the session, put him or her out of the studio, and tell them to go somewhere and learn the lyrics. Do not waste my time and my money. The ladies really resented it whenever I'd say my money.

"What! Oh, no he didn't! Just what do you mean your money? That's Berry Gordy, Jr.'s money, and your name is Mickey 'Jive Ass' Stevenson. You are not the president of Motown, okay? You're just the A&R man! That's all you are!"

I'd try to explain to the sistas that the money they wasted in the studio came out of my budget, but they were not hearing it. I was an asshole and a chauvinist pig, and that was that! Just between you and me, I would have loved to have had a female producer who could make hit records. Can you imagine the publicity we could've gotten out of that? But every time I tried a female producer, she would get into an argument with the musicians, or with the engineer, or even with the artists, over everything but the production. The session would start off like it was really gonna be something, but it would end up sounding like shit. I'd cut it off and put them out, and they'd curse me out. They would go straight to the chairman, B. G., with their complaints.

If you worry about what people think and say about you, take it from me, you'll end up stressed out, with high blood pressure and a bleeding ulcer.

Not me! I stayed in good health because I paid no attention to any of it. I was focused on my job and I loved it. If somebody didn't like the way I ran things in the A&R department, and their name wasn't B.G. Berry Gordy, Jr., they had a problem.

I'm proud to say that Motown kept as many as eight hit songs on the charts, Urban Network, Billboard and Cashbox magazine. The chairman was very happy with my way of doing things.

Like he said, "That's your department, and you're the man!"

And the hits just kept on coming.

GIFTS & GOODIES

Being streetwise came in handy every now and then. Once, for example, the promotion department needed some assistance in getting some ladies of the evening. I'm talking about some fine brown frames to be escorts, if you will, for some radio programmers we were hosting.

The DJs (disk jockeys) and programmers came from all over the country. The ladies we picked had to know how to show these boys a memorable good time. Imagine how crazed and outraged some of the ladies at the company were when they heard that Mickey Stevenson the A&R asshole was involved with procuring party girls. They thought it was just disgraceful! The fact is there were only a few people in the record company, artists included, who knew how the product even got on the air. Some didn't care how it got on, and the rest were completely oblivious. Take it from me, it took more than just having a hit piece of product, and you can take that to the bank.

The promotion department would use money, girls, vacations, whatever it took, even the artist if the radio station requested them for a show. Call it payola, call it doing favors, call it whatever you like, but back in the day, the record companies who knew how to keep the disc jockeys and program directors happy called it "getting a record on the radio, and keeping it there." Okay? Ladies of the evening and other gifts and goodies were required to make that happen.

These gifts and goodies traveled to cities from New York to California. Even in Detroit, the home of Motown, a package of goodies was required. The name of the game was the same everywhere. We were living in a time that demanded creative methods to get any Black artist's record played on pop radio stations everywhere in this country. Trust me; it took everything the promotion department could think of to make that happen, which included all of the above and more. It was impossible without the goodies.

We are talking about the '60s, which was a time in America when the bigots and hate groups all over this country were locked in a frightening, hateful state of mind. This psychopathic hatred included all Blacks, every man, woman, and child. Even the Jews and Hispanics couldn't escape the hatred.

We had George Lincoln Rockwell's Nazis boldly marching in the streets, openly opposing Blacks and Jews. One of their main targets was Dr. Martin Luther King and his fight for civil rights. Meanwhile, FBI chief J. Edgar Hoover's obsession with Dr. King made him determined to pull the good reverend down anyway he could. In the process, Hoover and the FBI simply turned a blind eye to injustices throughout the South, where Black and White civil rights workers were being beaten with baseball bats, viciously attacked by dogs and murdered - where churches were being burned as innocent children died in the fires. Not to mention the arrogant Southern governor and his storm troopers.

We saw the ones who stood in front of an all-white school with guns in hand, to make sure that no Black kids would enter the school. As they boldly defied the Supreme Court's ruling for school integration, Southern politicians in Washington D. C., (I'm talking about the good old boys) were openly opposed to integration but secretly dedicated to segregation. It was on their lips and in their hearts.

I'm just sayin' when you add all of that up, America was in a hell of a state of racial turmoil, but in the midst of all this ugliness was Motown Records.

The Music of Young America was helping to pull together people of all nationalities with the healing sound of music.

And the hits just kept on coming... Thank God!

UNION MATTERS

The musicians union in Detroit came down on Motown Records for recording music without a proper agreement with the union. As a matter of fact, we had no agreement with the union. It wasn't our fault; the union didn't consider Motown a part of the music world. The union had no interest in us whatsoever. We were just "a bunch of Negroes making some of those R & B records," which wasn't even considered real music in its estimation. As long as we didn't bother anybody or get outta hand, who cared?

I don't know exactly how it happened, but I do know that the musicians union out of New York gave the Detroit branch a call and advised it to get on the ball. In other words, wake the hell up and pay that Motown Records a visit. Not having Motown in the union was costing them a lot of money. They woke up! Uh uh! The Detroit branch gave Berry Gordy a polite call to say it was sending its union man around to have a meeting with him.

Berry told me, "You take the meeting; this is your department, so you handle it."

"No problem." I said.

I did my homework and soon found out who the union would send as the token Black brother. I dug a little deeper and found that the brother had a hearty appetite for the ladies. So I invited him out for an evening with me and a couple of fascinating ladies who could perform the art of fellatio so well, they could turn a grown man into a crybaby. You can take my word for that. Okay!

After a couple of meetings with the union brother, I was able to convince him to work with us. I wanted him to stay out of my way, so that I could continue recording my sessions without any interference, and we'd take good care of him.

Even he could see Motown was growing, and that meant the recording sessions would only get longer. Motown Records could become Detroit's largest source of income for the musicians union. I explained to him that he would no longer be the union's token Black, but a power player. I gave him my word that Motown would cover his back when that time came.

We made an arrangement that went like this - each time he came by the studio to check on us, the ladies would be waiting to take him out for dinner and a real good time. You get my drift? By the time he got back to the studio, everything would be over. He'd get a couple of session contracts to take back to the union, and everybody would be happy.

Motown was growing fast! We started cutting more and more sessions, day and night. I took on a horn section under Hank Cosby, who was a good arranger and saxophonist, as well as Beans Boles, who was also great on the baritone sax. I made Hank my assistant, and Beans his assistant. I was on a roll, baby!

Now picture this. I got Hank Cosby, Beans Boles and horns in the middle, with the sweet vocals of Louvain Demps, Jackie Hicks, Marlene Barrow-Tate and The Andantes' background on the top, with The Funk Brothers holding it all together. The sound was hot! The voices of those fantastic ladies, by the way, could be heard on everyone's records from Marvin Gaye to The Four Tops, The Supremes and everyone in between. According to Motown Museum's Allen Rawls, The Andantes were Motown's secret weapon; equivalent to The Funk Brothers. And Allen is absolutely right! I gotta tell you, I really loved those ladies. They were always on time, always in tune and as sweet as can be. They were an A&R Man's dream. Now moving right along, the producers, the writers and the artist all loved the way I stacked the different layers of sound, and why not? It was great! But to me, it still was not all together, not yet! Almost but not yet! You know the feeling you get when something is not quite right? Like something is missing? That's how I felt.

At first I couldn't put my finger on it. Then it hit me! Strings, violins and things! That's what we needed; our own string section to make it complete. Yeah! The best string players in Detroit were in the Detroit Symphony Orchestra, of course, so that's where I started to look for my string players. They're musicians, right?

I knew they could use some money like everybody else. Wrong! I walked into a wall of resistance. It was a ridiculous combination of prejudice, pomposity and stupidity. I'm talking about string players unwilling to work with Motown because we were a Black company, and they didn't want to associate themselves with R&B music.

Now try this on for size! The few highbrow Black string players, and I do mean a few, were afraid that if they were caught recording for Motown, they would lose their standing with the symphony, as if they had a standing in the first place. The rest of the sophisticated symphony players did not consider Motown music real music. I'd like to have seen them tell that to the millions buying the records, including some of their own kids. Okay?

I finally met one violinist, Gordon, who was a white second string player with the symphony, which meant he seldom got a chance to play. Gordon had a family, thank God! And I think he was more afraid of poverty than he was of working for Black people. For whatever reason, he decided to take a chance and work with us. All the string sessions had to be late at night. Since I had the union brother under control, the night time was the right time. Needless to say, it turned out to be the best decision Gordon ever made. When I added the string section to our productions, it gave the producers and writers a chance to add another dimension to their creativity. The strings also made us all stretch our creative minds to the limit. Let me explain what I mean by that.

At this time in our lives, not one of the producers or songwriters could read or write a note of music, and that included me! All of the sounds you heard, the notes, the beats, the words and music, were the sounds inside our heads, our hearts, and our souls. Some of us could put a few chord sheets together and play a little piano, but that was as good as it got. Writing string parts was out of the question. That meant Gordon, the violinist, really had his work cut out for him. Boy did he ever! Not only did he have to listen to all the string melodies and parts as we sang them in his ear, but he had to write them down the way we heard them. And that was with a lot of soul, baby! Gordon told me he needed more string players to make this work. He could get some of his friends from the symphony who were in need of work, but they didn't want any union trouble.

"Have you had any union problems since you've been working with us?" I asked him.

"No, I have not!" he said.

"Well then," I said, "the other players won't, either. You just get the other players and leave the union to me."

Gordon convinced four of his friends from the symphony, who obviously needed the work, to join us. The five of them played all the parts. They would double, triple, and even quadruple the parts to make it a full string section. With the amount of sessions we were doing day and night, it wasn't long before the string players were raking in some money, baby. It wasn't long before all the other players from the symphony wanted to work with Motown. I made Gordon the man over the string players, and every string player who wanted to play with Motown, Black or white, had to go through him. He was the man. With his help we all learned more about writing and arranging. He and his family became part of the Motown family.

As Motown grew, the union brother became very important, just as I told him he would. Matter of fact, the brother became too important for some of his union bosses. Here we go again with that racist bullshit. The union decided to demote the brother and put someone else in his position. Wrong! I couldn't let that happen. First of all, I had given the brother my word that Motown would cover his back. For another thing, a new man in his spot meant I would have to start all over again. I didn't have the time or the temperament for all that bullshit. The chairman got wind of the potential union problem and asked me if I needed any help. I told him I could handle it.

"Are you sure?" he asked. "This could get outta hand."

"I'm sure, B.G. I got this!"

I set up a meeting with the union bosses. When I walked into the conference room, I didn't see the brother or any other Blacks in the room for that matter.

There were six white guys all smoking cigars, drinking, and pretending to be talking to each other. Some of them looked like they'd had a little too much to drink, if you ask me. Hell, it was only one o'clock in the afternoon.

I apologized for being late and started right in, explaining that I'd just flown in from Chicago where I was looking over some recording studios for the company. "We don't want any trouble with the union here in Detroit," I said. "Our union brother here assured me that we had an understanding, an arrangement, so to speak, and that everybody was happy with it. By the way, where is he?" They gave me some lame excuse that I ignored.

"He works well with us," I said. "It's a cultural thing, you know what I mean? We don't wanna lose that cultural thing. Are you with me here? We're a Black company and we're proud of that here at home, and that's a good thing for everybody. Now if there's a problem here, we could start cutting more sessions in another city like Chicago maybe, or someplace where everybody can get along. Look, you guys, Detroit is our home too,

84

Motown, motor town, you see what I mean?"

The union boss jumped in with a big smile on his face. "Hey Mick, Mick! Slow down, brother, ha ha. Can I call you brother? See, we're all family here like you said, right? Everything is fine. This whole thing was a misunderstanding. That's why we called this meeting, to straighten everything out. Everything stays just like it is, right?"

Everybody agreed. "Right!" as we all shook hands.

"This is great, fellows," I said. "Have the brother give me a call when he's back in his office, and you all have a great day."

Not only did the union brother keep his position but they gave him a bigger office and a nice raise. He was now making enough money to pay for his own expensive relationships with the ladies. I got Bill Kaybush, the owner of the Twenty Grand nightclub where we booked some of our artists, to send the union bosses a case of good wine, and they loved it.

By the time we bought our third building, Motown Records was turning into a melting pot of race, creeds, and colors. We were the first true rainbow coalition in Detroit.

Did everybody love everybody? I can't answer that question, but I can tell you this without a doubt! They all loved Motown Records and what it stood for.

The pride it gave us all, Black and white, was phenomenal. Creating the music, The Motown Sound; that was the inspiration, in and of itself.

It took all of us to make that happen. That's the motivation that held us all together, making us truly One.

THE MISSING/CHECK THIS OUT

Now with all of this Motown love going around, everybody singing the company song, the huggin' and kissin' and stuff like that there goin' on, I want you to know that none of this brotherly love let me off the hook. What I mean is; I was still considered by some as the Black sheep of the Motown family. Whenever something was missing or misplaced, guess who they came to? Yours truly! And when someone needed to be found, fired, or straightened out, guess who would get the job? Yours truly!

I admit that because of my streetwise upbringing, I had to be in on everything or at least know something about it. Being questioned or accused all the time would drive some people crazy, but not me. Don't get me wrong. I didn't like it one bit, but I learned to ignore those incriminating remarks, and the people who made them.

I had my own cheering section, my own Amen Corner, with Smokey Robinson, Marvin Gaye, Barney Ales, the Tempts, and Martha Reeves - and when I add the one who signed my checks, Berry Gordy, Jr. to my list, what the hell? I was cool! The emotional struggle for me was like being on a roller coaster, up one day and down the next. After a while, you learn to roll with the punches, baby, you know what I mean?

I remember going to the studio one day feeling real good. This day was a very unusual day. We had recorded some great songs the night before, and between the sessions I had won a lot of money playing poker - so I was happy as a big dog. When I walked into the building, though, the whole place was in an uproar. Everybody stopped talking and looked at me. It was as if E. F. Hutton was giving away stock tips, only the looks they were giving me were like the ones they'd give a condemned man.

I stood there for a moment listening to the silence, then, working up an attitude, I said, "Okay people. I'm here, so what is the problem?"

Someone had stolen some company checks and forged the chairman's signature. That was the reason everyone was staring at me.

William R. had access to the checks, they whispered. In the A&R department, William R. writes at least a hundred checks a week. He could have easily slipped them in with his payroll, and no one would ever notice it. Yeah, that's right. You know he's friends with all those night life people, gamblers, hustlers, and don't forget the ladies of the evening.

That was the talk throughout the company. But not everyone was whispering; some thought I was guilty, period. Wait a minute, it gets worse!

When they called the company meeting and asked everyone to take a handwriting test, I refused. I told them that everybody knows I signed a hundred checks or more every week. "Go look at them," I said. "I'm not taking no test, no nothing." I walked out and went back to my office.

The ones who were suspicious spoke right up. "That just proves it! Slick Mick did it, or he had something to do with the missing checks."

It got so bad the chairman himself called me to his office to tell me I should at least take the lie detector test.

"For what?" I asked.

"It would let everyone here know that you didn't take that money," he answered.

I told him I wasn't concerned about what they thought; I was only interested in what he thought. "I don't work for them, I work for you."

That's when B.G. asked me straight out. "Did you take the checks?"

That took me by surprise. I don't know whether I felt hurt or disappointed, maybe both. I looked him in the eyes and I asked him, "Do you believe that I would steal checks or anything else from you, B.G.?"

With that familiar half-smile, half-smirk, he shook his head and said, "No!"

"Well, that answers your question, don't it?" I replied with a sense of relief we both felt.

As B.G. walked away, he said, "Go back to work."

For the first time since I had been with Motown, I was really bothered. I walked around Hitsville in a very strange mood. I guess you could call it being low in my spirit. If you've ever felt like that, you know it's hard to pull yourself out of it. Women go shopping for shoes or something, men go get drunk or have sex or both. My problem was I didn't feel like doing anything. On my way to the studio to check on the sessions, I happened to bump into Pop Gordy, Berry's father, coming down the stairs from my office. Pops would come through Hitsville all the time, fixing things or just walking through checking things out. When he saw the look on my face that day he asked me, "What's the matter?"

I told him, I wasn't feeling good, but I couldn't fool Pops. He could see right through that answer.

He put his hand on my shoulder, looked me in the eyes and said "You're doing a great job, son, that's all that matters."

The wisdom and honesty in his voice gave me a good feeling. He gave me this great big reassuring smile, with his white hair shining and penetrating eyes, and he walked away. His kindness released something in me. I decided to find out who took that money. It was definitely an inside job, and sooner or later somebody would start spending it. The finger pointers were right about one thing; I had a slew of buddies in the streets of Detroit who could do and would do anything for me. I asked my friends to keep an eye out for any unusual spending by anybody they knew to be connected with Motown. In the meantime, I watched everyone I could from within. You see, we played a lot of poker in those days, and for big bucks, too. I generally won, except when B.G. got in the game. The rest of the boys, like Harvey, Marvin, Holland-Dozier-Holland, even Smokey, they were no match for me.

I was looking for a player with some fresh money. Nobody showed up. Around this time, I had to go to New York to produce a session on the singing movie star, Tony Martin. The best thing about that was I had a chance to meet one of my idols of musical movies; his wife, Cyd Charisse.

She was an incredible dancer, with beautiful long legs. I fell in love with her when I saw her dance with Gene Kelly in Singin' in the Rain, one of my favorite musicals along with My Fair Lady, West Side Story, Oliver and along with my youngest daughter Taylor, our favorite musical of all time The Sound of Music.

When Taylor was around four years old, I collected all the great musicals like Oklahoma, The King and I, South Pacific, Carousel, and State Fair.

Every weekend my daughter and I would gather some snacks, make popcorn and get comfortable and watch those great musicals together. We'd watch them over and over again. By the time Taylor was around seven, she knew almost every song and every plot in all the movies. I surprised her and took her to see The Sound of Music on Broadway. Taylor was so excited to see this magnificent production live and on stage, she was almost in tears.

"Oh Daddy," she said "this is wonderful".

Throughout the play her eyes were lit up and her smile was so big I thought she was going to explode. When the cast started to sing her favorite song, she couldn't hold back any longer and burst out singing loud and clear along with the cast, "THESE ARE A FEW OF MY FAVORITE THINGS!"

Thank God it was toward the end of the song. When the applause began at the end of the song, some of the audience around us turned to Taylor and applauded her. She was so embarrassed she didn't know what to do.

On the way to the hotel she said, "Dad! (She calls me Dad when she wants something) I want to be in show business."

"You wanna what?" I said.

"You heard me. Dad, come on, I wanna do what they were doing on the stage, okay?"

She touched her heart and took a deep breath. "It was so exciting, Daddy, and I wanna learn about all of it."

Wow! I didn't know what to say. As I looked at her, all I could think about was my precious baby growing up. I collected my thoughts.

"There's no doubt about it, you are going to be in show business," I replied calmly.

At thirteen, Taylor won first place in Shakespeare's Taming of the Shrew, performed as a two-person humorous competition. At fifteen, she was working with her mom acting and stage managing a musical with a hundred performers in it. Along with going to school, she sings, writes, and also takes the time out to give me critique in some of my productions. Now is that exciting or what? We must be mindful about what we say and do with our young ones. Never forget that, good or bad, first impressions on the mind of a child can last forever!

Now let's get back to my meeting Cyd Charisse in person. It was a very special moment for me. She looked as vibrant in person as she did in the movies, not quite as tall, but twice as beautiful with that big gorgeous smile of hers. She was gracious and charming when she talked about how much she enjoyed the music of Motown.

Needless to say the meeting with Tony Martin went very well. Actually, I worked not only with Tony Martin but with a number of other singing movie stars. Let me bring you up to date on that.

The chairman came up with this great idea. It was a way to expand our label, broaden our horizons and diversify our audiences. In other words, we would incorporate more white folks, you feel me? We also recorded Barbara McNair, Diahann Carroll, Billy Eckstine and a few crossover artists.

We had an office in New York run by Raynoma Gordy. You remember Ray. She and the chairman were separated by this time, but they remained friends, at least friendly enough for B.G. to let her run the New York office. I had Mickey Gentile, a producer there, set up some sessions with Tony Martin.

Mickey Gentile was a Motown family writer, producer and a good hustler; one of the inside guys in the New York music scene. Mickey knew everybody. He even introduced me to Ashford and Simpson, who I fell in love with and wanted them for Motown – and told them that's where they should be. I offered Mickey Gentile the job as our East Coast Rep and he jumped at the opportunity. This was a dream come true for him. He was one proud Italian brother. Mickey told me that Billy Eckstine was in town and he had four singers with him that where great, "You gotta see them" he said with such passion, "they're really good!"

When we finished the session with Tony Martin, which was long and drawn out, I needed a break so Mickey took me to Jellies restaurant to eat and we sat in Frank Sinatra's private booth for dinner. Can you imagine that? Motown at Sinatra's table – that was hot!

After that we went to see Billy Eckstine at Basin Street, one of the coolest night spots in the city. I could hear these great voices as we walked in the club. Wow! The first thing I saw was these four guys on stage singing their asses off – to my surprise, Billy's opening act was The Four Tops!

I told you about seeing this group when they were known as The Four Aims. They were the ones who won the contest at the Warfield Theater. I was glad they'd changed their name to The Four Tops. There was already a white group called The Ames Brothers. I gotta tell you, The Four Tops sounded better than ever. They were great! I was so excited I couldn't wait for them to finish the show. I invited them over for a drink and started telling them about the first time I saw them in Detroit. I told them what they wore that night and I even described the Mr. B. shirts they wore. The thing that blew their minds was when I started singing the song they sang that night;

"Rock roll rock, everybody, Rock roll rock."

"I have to tell you fellas, that night I said to myself, 'these guys are gonna be great artists.' Man! Little did I know that I would be the one to make that happen for you."

They laughed and we talked for a long time. I told them how they'd been a heavy influence on my decision to get into this business. "Thanks to you," I said, "I am the A&R director of the hottest record company in the business, Motown. Now here we are in New York together. Faith has played a part in this whole thing right from the beginning. This is destiny, my brothers, straight up."

They couldn't believe it!

"Now you brothers need to come and see me soon as you get home," I went on. "I wanna sign you up and make some hit records." I must have talked the whole time; they hardly said a word. The Tops were just drinking and listening. I didn't know if I was getting through to them at all. It was time for them to do another set on stage. I gave them my card and told them to get in touch with me.

As I headed for the door, I turned to The Tops and started singing, "Rock roll rock everybody, rock roll rock." To my surprise, the Four Tops joined me and started singing it with me, blending in that great harmony of theirs. As I went out the door I could still hear them singing, "Rock roll rock everybody!" What a great sound, and what a great moment. Oh my God! I was so excited over seeing The Four Tops, I left without seeing Billy Eckstine.

I must've done a good job convincing them because when I got home two weeks later, I was surprised to see The Four Tops waiting for me. They came into my office and stood over my desk. Duke Fakir, the spokesman for the group, said,

"Mickey Stevenson, you said if we sign with you, you would make us some hit records, right? Well, we're here. Where are the contracts? We wanna look them over."

I said, "No problem, I have some right here. All of our contracts are the same for new artists." I reached in my drawer and gave each of them one. I said, "Take them to your lawyer and look them over. But I gotta tell you, we're not gonna change a thing. What we're gonna do is get you some hit records."

They stepped outside of my office and stayed for about thirty minutes. When they walked back in, Duke said, "We don't need no lawyer. Like you said, faith had a hand in this and we're putting our faith in your hands. Where do we sign?" They signed the contracts right then and there. It gets better; a mystery was about to be solved.

My friends on the street let me know that they saw the chairman's driver and his lady friend in an after-hours joint. She was sporting a new mink coat. I found that interesting, since none of the drivers around Motown made enough money to afford a mink anything, including my driver. Needless to say, when we checked it out we discovered that Berry's driver had stolen the checks and forged B.G.'s signature. He had done it while picking up the morning mail bags. The new checkbooks from the bank were in the mail bags. He pulled some checks from the bottom of the checkbooks and went to work forging them. After he confessed, my credibility went up a hundred and fifty percent.

Everyone in the company who had accused me was now trying to find creative ways to apologize. I played it off like it was no big deal and invited everyone to hear this new group we'd just signed.

By the time The Four Tops finished singing, every producer and writer in the place went to work on them, including me. Holland-Dozier-Holland came up with the hit Sugar Pie Honey Bunch. Then Ivy Jo and I hit them with Just Ask the Lonely. But H.D.H. came back with Bernadette and I'll Be There. The Tops never stopped!

And the hits just kept on coming.

THE MOTOR TOWN REVIEW

Ever heard of the Chitlin' Circuit? When we took the first "Motor Town Review" on tour, we went out on the Chitlin' Circuit. That's right, you heard it right; I said the Chitlin' Circuit. The Chitlin Circuit (named after the southern food staple Chiterlings), was a tour route of safe and neutral venues that Black entertainers could perform in freely and without harassment during the racial segregation era; and all the Black entertainers played that circuit.

It was one of the few tours where you could make money and sell a lot of records at the same time. Artists like Ray Charles, Aretha Franklin, the Isley Brothers, Al Green, Dinah Washington; all of them and more played and stayed on the circuit. They would play four and five shows a day, with seven or eight other acts on the show.

This is where the fans and the potential fans got a chance to get up close and personal with the artists, hang out at the same clubs, see them in the same restaurants eating some of the local southern fried chicken, black eyed peas with collard greens, chitlins and sweet cornbread. They'd have a chance to talk to the artists themselves about the personal ways the music affected or inspired them, how much they loved the artists songs and that their song was the reason mama's baby got here early. You know what I mean? Up close and personal. The Chitlin' Circuit was nothing to fool around with, though, and a new artist on the circuit better be good. Or else.

When the audience liked you, it was like being on a honeymoon with your first real love; they just couldn't get enough of your wonderful stuff. But if you were bad, the audience would boo your ass off the stage and send you home crying to your mama like a newborn baby. Now picture this; two thousand fans in the audience singing the words to your songs, right along with you and the artist. That's love, baby! It would take your emotions to another level. Smokey Robinson once said, "When I hear the fans singing my songs, I shout, turn it up! Turn it up!"

The Chitlin' Circuit tour would play a week at the Royal Theater in Baltimore and the Howard Theater in Washington D. C., then move on to the Uptown in Philly, and right up to New York's world famous Apollo Theater. They would close the tour out at the Regal in Chicago. Sometimes they'd finish up at home, at the Fox Theater or the Greystone Ballroom in Detroit.

Most of the Motown artists were young and right out of the 'hood. Most of them had never traveled any further than their church picnics; to say they were inexperienced would be putting it mildly. The majority of them had never performed on a real stage before. They had performed at places like high school gyms, doing their thing in front of friends and neighbors, which does not compare to performing on a real stage in front of thousands. We had our work cut out for us. We had to prepare them for the real stage, the talk shows, radio and TV, you name it. We had to build their confidence and self-esteem.

The chairman formed his own artist development department to help groom the artists. B.G. put his sister Esther Gordy Edwards in charge, assisted by his brother- in-law Harvey Fuqua, and me. He also formed a management company. This way we could protect the artists from outside managers interfering with the development of the Motown artists. Esther was very elegant and extremely intelligent. She was married to one of Detroit's politicians, George Edwards, so she was very well schooled in the protocol of political parties and the who's who in Detroit.

Esther and I got along very well. She liked me from the very beginning; why, I don't know. I came to the company with a streetwise mentality, but like the chairman, Esther saw something that made her take the time to work with me.

I must admit I learned quite a few things from Esther over the years. She shared with me a lot of her savvy and sophistication, like how to dress properly for meetings, what colors were more impactful, where to sit in meetings to get the most attention, all things of which I had no prior knowledge. Her wisdom helped me throughout my career.

One of Esther's most valuable qualities was the way she nurtured the artists. She had this foster mother thing going for her. It would draw the artists to her like a magnet; her motherly instinct for the girls was very strong. The female artists would come to Esther with their problems, personal and otherwise, and believe me; they all had problems, mostly boys, if you ask me. Esther would solve their problems or give them good sound advice. B .G. put Esther in charge of taking the artists out on the first "Motown Review." Knowing the kind of respect and control I had with the artists and the musicians, she wanted me to help her with the tour. Personally I hated the damn tours, not because of the trips but because I'm not an artist, and it would only be extra work for me. Plus, it would take me away from the things I did best, running the A&R department. That's where

I belonged, that's where I was happiest, and that's where I made my money. I did not relish the idea of running around the country in some damn uncomfortable bus, babysitting a group of young artists. Not me. I was not interested.

When Esther called and asked me to go out with the Motown tour, I told her I didn't think I'd be able to because of my heavy workload, sessions, deadlines, you name it. She listened very patiently in her sophisticated way and said she understood and she'd talk with me later. Ten minutes later, B.G. called to tell me I was going out with the tour. He said one of us would have to go. He couldn't, so that left me. He explained how important it was that this tour be successful, and he knew I could help make that happen. Berry always had a way with words. The man knew how to make you feel needed, as if things wouldn't work without you. After talking with B.G., not only did I want to go, but I was going to make sure that The Motown Review came off better than any show out there. And there were some hot shows on the Chitlin' Circuit; the Ray Charles revue, James Brown, Joe Tex with his Skinny Legs and All revue, Harold Melvin and the Blue Notes, Curtis Mayfield and the Impressions, Sam and Dave, the O' Jays, and more. If an artist had a good record - notice I did not say a hit record - they would be on somebody's tour promoting it.

There was Gene Chandler (better known as the Duke of Earl), Jerry Butler, Chuck Jackson, Ben E. King, Lloyd Price and his big band, and the ladies of soul, Aretha Franklin, The Sweet Inspirations, Dionne Warwick, and need I go on?

All the shows out there were good; some better than others, of course. But to me, there was something missing from most of the shows. The artists were great, the songs were hot, but something wasn't doing it for me. After working some of the greatest rooms and seeing some of the best shows in the world, I wanted to bring some of that knowledge to our show. Since I was going to take the Motown show out, I wanted it to be the best. I watched some of the show, trying to put my finger on it. And then it hit me! Most of the artists appearing on the shows had their own musicians, backup singers and band equipment onstage. When their time was up, the stagehands had to run out onstage, remove the instruments and replace them with the instruments of the next act. They even had to bring out platforms, place them in certain positions on the stage according to each artist's specifications, and reset the mics, the whole nine yards.

Now believe me, this process could take even longer when the artists' egos got involved. Some of the changes took so long you could eat a hot dog, a box of popcorn, two candy bars, drink a soda, even go to the restroom, and you'd still have at least ten more minutes to wait. Some tours would have a comedian tell jokes while the stagehands set up the next act. Even the comedian would run out of things to say. Some of the comedians were great and their careers grew because of their appearances on the Chitlin' Circuit. Comedians like Richard Pryor, Moms Mabley, Nipsey Russell, Winehead Willie, and others. In case you're wondering about Redd Foxx, he was already knockin' 'em dead doing his own thing on the night club circuit.

Some of the touring shows would use the theater house band. The problem with that was if you didn't have a big hit record or a big name, you got very little or no rehearsal time at all, which meant some of the new artists got the "boo" treatment from the audience the moment they hit the stage, and that was a sad thing to see. Artists like Ray Charles, James Brown and Sam and Dave would bring their own bands, which in most cases were the musicians they recorded with, so they would sound just like their records. The Motown artists had so many different singers with all kinds of music. So I decided the best thing to do was to tour with our own orchestra as well, calling them the Motown Orchestra. I pulled most of the musicians out of the studio. Why not? I wasn't going to be recording until after the tour anyway. It also would solve the problem of the producers cutting product on artists without my permission.

The only other problem I had would be my drummer, Benny Benjamin. How in the hell was I gonna keep up with Benny on the road? That would be impossible. Benny could find drugs in a closet if you left him there long enough. I couldn't take him with us; that was out of the question. I decided to put two of my best street guys on Benny. They would keep me informed about everything he did and every place he went. I didn't want anyone to take advantage of him while I was gone, you feel me? I took a backup drummer, Richard "Pistol" Allen, with us on the tour.

While the artists worked on their performances, the band rehearsed the show in the studio like a session. This went on day and night, until all the artists and the music sounded exactly like the records, sometimes even better! I was at every rehearsal, and by the time we finished, I knew every song and every tempo from beginning to end. That's when Smokey asked me to conduct the orchestra for the tour. "No one knows the tempos and feelings of the songs like you, William R.," he said. And he said it with conviction! All the artists agreed with Smokey that I should be the conductor.

I remember conducting a band every night on the road with the Hamptones, and it was never the same band. This time I got the Funk Brothers and my own horn section. It's all about tempos, intros, and endings. I had memorized every song, so between me and the Funk Brothers, I figured this should be a walk in the park. We had a great show. I even had the main background singers, the Andantes with me, singing on the off stage mic keepin' it real! I gotta tell you, they also helped make the sound of Motown. I had to have them on the mic to keep it real. My other background singers were the Vandellas, the Marvelettes, the Tops, and the Tempts. Even the Miracles, Mary Wells and Kim Weston got into the act.

You see, each time an artist exited the stage after doing his or her own act they would go to one of the offstage mics and help sing background for the artists going onstage. Whoever was available and knew the songs would lend a hand, better yet, lend a voice. Everyone knew everybody's songs. The Motown Review had plenty of love going around. It was great!

The Motown tour was turning out to be a winner. We got a chance to expose our new artists to huge audiences, and a chance to move some records as we unveiled the Motown sound and image to thousands of new fans. And it was running smooth!

But when we opened the tour in Washington DC, the damn tour was turning out to be a financial bust right from the start. I couldn't figure it out. We had a full house at every show. I'm talking about people standing in the aisles, and still we were not making any money. It was driving me crazy! We were working our asses off, doing four and five shows a day.

Here we were, playing to packed houses with long lines outside, cars pulling up in front of the theater, people grabbing up any available tickets, and still we were not making any money! At this point, my street savvy kicked in. Okay, Mickey, somebody is ripping us off. Who could it be? It was just before another show started that Smokey called me to his dressing room. He looked a little concerned.

"Hey, Mickey," he said. "Every time I go out on stage, I see the same girls' faces in the first four rows. They have been there since the first show, man, singing the songs before I even get to them. They know the whole show by heart."

I didn't understand what the hell he was talking about, so he took me to the curtain and pointed them out to me. "Look," he said. "Right there, see, those are the same girls sitting in the same seats."

"Oh shit!" It hit me like a ton of bricks. Now I knew why we weren't making any money. The people weren't moving! The same audience was sitting in the same seats throughout every show. The people in the lines outside the theater weren't buying the tickets; they had already bought their tickets. They were waiting in line to get into the theater. Only a few people were getting in after each show, because only a few were going out. I got this great idea and ran straight to the theater box office. I told them not to sell any more tickets before the next show started. The orchestra was about to start the overture for the show when I walked onstage.

"Ladies and gentlemen," I announced. "Everyone in the theater will see a complete show. There's a line of people waiting outside, friends, relatives, and neighbors of yours. They all bought tickets just like you did. Now they would appreciate it if you would leave the theater at the end of this performance, so that your friends and relatives may come in the theater and enjoy the Motown review. I thank you for your cooperation." The audience applauded when I shouted, "its show time!"

When the show was over, I couldn't believe it! After that wonderful pleading speech I had made, I just knew they would leave the theater after the show. Boy was I wrong! Only a few people left the theater, and they were the older ones. The rest of them just sat there. They weren't even thinking about moving. That's when I had the house lights turned up. I grabbed some security guards, and we walked down every aisle in that theater, removing people and escorting them out. We were pulling people out from under seats, behind seats, chasing them out of the bathrooms, from behind the balcony curtains. They were everywhere, hiding in the damndest places. If they could find a place to hide, they did. It was crazy! Some of them were not too happy about being put out of the theater either, and told me so in no uncertain terms.

Baltimore, Maryland, was next, and we were playing the Royal Theater. To start with, Baltimore in the '60s and '70s was known for having the roughest Black audiences on the Chitlin' Circuit. I'm talkin' about rude, wild, rowdy dowdy audiences. Now, if they liked you, they'd scream and holler until the cows came home. But if they didn't like you, look out, baby! What I didn't know was they could also be very violent.

Before the show started I walked out on the stage and did my speech about everyone leaving the theater right after the show. Well, the same thing happened; very few people left the theater. This time as the security guards and I were removing people from everywhere and escorting them out of the theater, some of them started shouting and pointing at me,

"We'll see you when the show is over, nigga, yeah! We'll be waiting on yo ass outside, yeah brother man, you gotta ass whoopin' coming! We're gonna kick yo Black ass!"

They were loud and mad as hell. Everyone in the theater heard them, including the artists, the band, everybody. I played it off by paying them no attention. I just kept putting everybody out until I had cleared the theater for the next show. I gotta tell you, deep down inside I knew I had a problem working this city. After each show as I cleared the theater, the threats got worse. As the night went on and we were into the last show of the evening, I started looking around to see who I could count on to help me out of the problem I'd be faced with in less than an hour. I gotta tell ya, the prospects didn't look too good.

There were the Four Tops, Smokey and the Miracles, and a few band members. That was it. The others I couldn't count on and the rest were girls. I thought about getting some of the artists to help me, but if any of them got hurt I would have trouble with Berry Gordy and everyone else at the company, trying to explain how I got the artists all beat up. The band members could help me, but if they got hurt, the show went down the drain.

As I stood there thinking about my options and how I was gonna handle this ass-whoopin' I was about to get, I could see all the artists and the band members packing up and getting on the bus. When the bus pulled off for the hotel with the last of the show members on it, I found myself alone, with only the security guards. At least that's what I thought, until I looked around for them. What the hell? Even the security guards had split. I was on my own.

Now I really got scared. I'd been in gang fights before but never by myself. I was gonna have to take this ass whoopin' alone. I looked out of the back door window to see if the gang bangers were out there. My God, there must have been twenty of them, male and female. Some were there to kick my ass, and the others were there to watch me get my ass kicked. They knew I hadn't come out because they'd checked the windows of the buses and cars that had pulled off. Yes, I thought about calling the police. But that was a no-no! That would have been the worst thing in the world to do. I would have pissed the gang bangers off even more in those days, and in Baltimore, Maryland, forget about it. For one, if the police showed up at all, they probably would've just sat in their cars, eating donuts and drinking coffee, while they watched the reality show of me getting my ass whipped. "Let the niggers kill each other."

I knew I couldn't stay in the theater all night. I had to come out some time. After stalling as long as I could, I decided to get it over with. I took a deep breath, crossed my heart and opened the back door. When they saw me, everybody stopped talking and started staring. I stepped outside the door and looked around. It looked like the crowd had grown even bigger. Man, was I in for it. Nobody moved, they just stood there looking at me, waiting to see what I was gonna do. I took another deep breath and headed straight for my car. I didn't run. I walked, and they just watched. I knew I wasn't gonna make it but it was worth a try. That's when I heard this voice. It was a girl's voice.

"Mickey, Mickey Stevenson, Mickey, I know you hear me calling you, nigga. It's me, Dottie."

Dottie? I said to myself, I don't know any Dottie. But that voice sounded familiar. It sounded like... Baby Doll, the booster I knew back in Detroit. I took a chance and shouted back, "Baby Doll, is that you?"

"Yeah! It's me, fool!" she said as she started walking towards me with her friend, a very big man. "They don't call me Baby Doll around here. They know me as Dottie. That's my real name."

She turned to her friend, who was holding her hand, and said, "Baby, Mickey is the one that got me outta that trouble, you know, when I was in Detroit, remember with the police and everything?"

The big guy - and I do mean big! - had the most outsized muscles I've ever seen. He looked like a Black Terminator with long straight hair that was soaked in some kinda oil and dripping all over his T-shirt. This crazy look appeared on his face,

"That's him?"

Trying to get him to remember, Baby Doll said, "Yeah! Don't you remember, I told you 'bout him? That's the Mickey I was talking' bout, paid for my airline ticket, I told you."

He said, "The song writer dude?"
Baby Doll shook her head yes, happy she was finally getting through.

"Yeah, baby! He was the one who knew that cop and the whole thing." She kept saying," That's what I'm talkin' bout, that's him."

Her friend the terminator, with that crazy look on his face, started rubbing his hands like he was thinking about what he was going to do to me. "So that's the nigga right there, huh?"

Baby Doll, with her hands on her hips and a smile on her face, said once again, "Yeah, that's the brother!"

All of a sudden, he raised his fist up over my head then brought it down real slow and he hit me on the shoulder softly. "Wow! Brother Man. That was some good lookin' out." He gave me a hard high five. "Good lookin' out, bro!" He turned to the crowd and said, "Hey, ya'll! The brother's all right! He's down with me all the way. You hear what I'm saying? He saved my woman's ass from doing some real time." Everybody started giving me the high five and shaking my hand like I was some kinda hero! As it turned out, Baby Doll's friend, Bubba, was "the man," the ringleader, and what he said was it. Not only did Baby Doll - I mean Dottie - save my ass, but she and Bubba followed me to my hotel for drinks. Dottie even offered to pay back the money I gave her for the airline ticket. I told her she already had!

Bubba shook his head, "Naw man. I pay my debts, right baby?"

Dottie smiled and rubbed his face, "We sure do baby."

That's when I said, "Well I could use a favor."

"What is it?" he asked, "What favor you talkin' about?"

"I could use you and a couple of your boys to be my security guards for a few days. I'll pay you to help me." I replied.

Bubba looked at me like I had lost my mind and shouted "Security Guards? Cops? You want us to be the Police?!" He started laughing out loud "Haaa ha ha ha!" And then he leaned in close to me and said real soft, "Can I wear one of those security jackets with the word Police on it?"

I whispered back, "You sure can!"

Bubba jumped back all excited and gave me a hard high five as he hollered "Alright then!"

By the time we finished getting high, I had hired Bubba and some of his boys to be my security guards for the remainder of the week in Baltimore.

When we walked into the theater the next day, I immediately fired those two jive ass security guards who'd left me high and dry. And I made them leave the security jackets with the word Police on them. From that day on, I had no more trouble with clearing the audiences. I started hiring the boys from the 'hood in every city, and the audience exchange went as smooth as silk. So did the Motown reviews. The show started making money and selling records.

When the tour reached the Apollo in New York, I remember going to the theater early. I must have stood in that theater-lobby for an hour or more just looking at the hand-painted portraits on the walls; portraits of all the great artists who had appeared there.

They were in brilliant colors and in my mind, I placed the names with each face, and the portraits seemed to just come alive. I could even hear the songs that made them famous in my head. It was eerie. It felt like the artist who had painted the portraits at the Moulin Rouge in Las Vegas, had lent his hands and his spirit to the artist here in New York. That spiritual connection helped make these portraits at the Apollo come alive as well. Like the Moulin Rouge, the portraits were on both sides of the lobby walls. It was like a giant never ending mirror, preserving these great talented artists forever. As I walked through the lobby into the theater, I began to feel the energy of all the artists who had played the Apollo, including my mother.

I felt my eyes tear up and a lump grow in my throat, as I stepped out on that empty stage. It was my mom!

All I could think about was my mom.

Momma had always wanted us to be in show business. Standing on that stage brought back memories, memories of when I was a kid. I could see it; even feel it like it was yesterday.

My mother, Kitty "Brown Gal" Stevenson, with me and my brothers right here, on this stage, appearing on amateur night at the Apollo Theater.

As I stood there frozen in time, I could hear the crowd screaming and hollering for us. My God! It was a magical moment reappearing. I could see my mother smiling at me. She's right over there, with tears in her eyes.

104

"Hey, Momma, I know you're here! I'm here too, right here at the Apollo Theater, and I'm onstage too! Momma! I'm not singing this time, but Momma, I'm standing here and I'm in show business."

I couldn't hold back the tears any longer.

"Momma, I'm working with a great company. You would really like them. And guess what, Momma? Like you, I'm writing songs, hit songs, too! I'm producing records and everything. And that thing you taught me about staying focused, I do it, I do it all the time. Oh, Momma, I never had the chance to say thank you, thank you Momma, and I love you, I love you and I miss you very much, very much."

The Motown review was a huge success at the Apollo, so successful we had to add extra shows. We broke the market wide open and sold a lot of records.

And the hits just kept on coming.

MARVIN GAYE

Have you ever met someone you felt you've known before, like in another life or something? That's just the way it was with Marvin and me. We were soul mates from day one. When the chairman brought Marvin Gaye to me, it was at a time when I was up to my neck with young, naïve but very enthusiastic artists, mostly girls. So Marvin Gaye was a breath of fresh air. We connected instantly!

Marvin came off as very sincere. "I'm very glad to meet you, William R.," he said. "I hope you don't mind me calling you that."

"Hey, it works for me, Marv."

"It's gonna be a pleasure working with you, William R., I can feel it."

He said that with such conviction I didn't know what to say. All I know is we became friends, very close friends, like brothers even. I found out why he was so glad to meet me. I was obviously put in his path for a reason. To enlighten you in detail about my relationship with Marvin as an artist, a writer and a friend, I have to start with his friend, Harvey Fuqua. Harvey was what the ladies called tall, dark and handsome. He was the lead singer, songwriter, producer and co-owner of the Moonglows. They were a pretty hot doo wop group. They had some hit R&B songs out like Secret Love, Sincerely and The Ten Commandments of Love.

The doo wop sound was beginning to phase out, and due to a misunderstanding between Harvey and Bob Lester, a member of the group and co- owner, they decided to go their separate ways, each forming their own group of Moonglows. This is where Marvin Gaye comes in. You see, Harvey was working with this young group of singers called the Marquees whose lead singer was Marvin. Harvey took Marvin and the group under his wing, changing their name to Harvey and the Moonglows.

The doo wops were fading faster and the gigs were coming even slower. After a recording with Etta James that didn't happen, Harvey tried a few recordings with his Moonglows featuring Marvin Gaye, but that didn't happen either. Nothing was working; it was time to move on.

So in 1960, Harvey left Chess Records in Chicago. He and Marvin Gaye came to Detroit to join Anna Records, a new label run by Gwen and Anna

Gordy, Berry Gordy's sisters. Harvey Fuqua became the A&R man for Anna Records and Marvin became an artist on the label. Marvin Gaye was also the session drummer for Anna Records, and he was a damn good drummer, I might add. Stay with me now; this is important.

In spite of all of Harvey's Moonglow experience, his ear for music and eye for talent like Marvin Gaye, The Spinners, Jr. Walker & the All Stars, Johnny Bristol and others, over a year and a half had gone by and Anna Records was not happening at all. Did you get that? It's not that Harvey wasn't good. He was just unlucky.

The only thing that was growing in this picture was the love affair between Gwen Gordy and Harvey Fuqua. Now that was on fire and going so strong they got married! The failing Anna Records label was - to put it gently - absorbed, merged, taken over by their brother Berry Gordy, Jr.

Everything and everybody at Anna went to the Tamla label, a Motown subsidiary line. Up to this point I had very little interaction with Marvin Gaye or Harvey, for that matter.

I had my hands full running Motown's A&R department and destroying my personal life in the process, but I loved it, what can I tell you! Harvey and Marvin were busy doing their thing on the Tamla label. Now Marvin had his dream. He saw himself as the next great crooner, a Nat King Cole, Andy Williams, or even a Black Frank Sinatra.

Harvey and Marvin had recorded two or three albums with that crooner concept and released a couple of singles on Marvin as well. The first album was The Soulful Moods of Marvin Gaye. Now you know they were trippin.' Nobody knew who Marvin Gaye was, nobody but a few fans including his family, Harvey Fuqua, Gwen Gordy Fuqua and Marvin's soon- to-be-wife Anna Gordy. The other loser was an album of Broadway standards and jazz songs. It gets worse. Throw in some singles like Mr. Sandman and Let Your Conscience Be Your Guide, and you gotta whole lotta nothing happening with Marvin Gaye, nothin' but some money going out of the window.

The songs were too soft! Too poppy, too Broadway and not enough soul, baby! Brother Marvin was going to have to put that idea on ice until he got some hit records under his belt. Okay! Boosting Marvin's ego and hanging on to his every word was Anna Gordy. Anna was fine, and I do mean fine. She was tall with a great shape, long legs and very sexy. She was a little older than Marvin, and a lot smarter. Did I say she was smart? Sorry, I meant very smart. As a matter of fact, all the Gordy sisters were fine, sexy and very smart. Gwen and Anna Gordy would take a brother's breath away when they walked by, and I'm a witness to that.

By now, everyone could see that Anna Gordy and Marvin had a thing going on hot and heavy. Anna's belief in him was a plus for Marvin. You see, Anna had a lot of influence with her brother, Berry Gordy. Remember I told you B. G. loved his sisters and was willing to do just about anything to please them. That included going along with some product on Marvin Gaye that was not happening at all. Why B.G. went along with this crooning idea for as long as he did was beyond me. My opinion is it was because of his sista Anna.

Marvin, being the stubborn kinda fellow that he was, had a real fixation on making this crooner thing work. Anna Gordy was going right along with him. We all know how crazy love is. It will make you see anything you wanna see, and believe anything you wanna believe, you see what I'm saying? Now that's my personal opinion and since this is my book, I can tell it like I saw it, and that's just what I'm doing. Okay!

Even Berry's empathy and his patience with Marvin and his sister had its limits. That's when B.G. brought Marvin Gaye to meet me; it meant the chief had finally reached that limit. With his trademark half-grin, Berry looked at me and said, "I want a hit record on him." He turned Marvin Gaye over to me and walked away.

It came off like some kinda joke, but I knew the chief was as serious as a heart attack. As I introduced myself to Marvin, I said, "Okay, chief, I got this." Marvin was shaking my hand like he'd finally found the one person who was gonna focus on him, and help him get his dream off the ground. The A&R man of Motown, William R. By the way, Marvin started calling me William R. from day one. We hit it off right from the start.

I loved being in the Hitsville U. S. A. building, it didn't matter where, in the recording studio or in one of the rehearsal rooms. The place just had a creative energy in it, that you could feel from the moment you entered the building. We all had the same feeling about the place we called Hitsville. Every one of us, including Smokey Robinson, Ivy Jo Hunter, Holland-Dozier-Holland, songwriter/producer Norman Whitfield, even Marvin loved being there. Nobody wanted to go home, we were at home!

Every chance I'd get I would jump on a piano and work on a song. Marvin would watch me create and after he'd heard enough he would say,

"Will you get off the piano, William R., and let me work on the song for a while?"

Just between you and me, Marvin couldn't stand my piano playing. I couldn't blame him; I was terrible with a capital T and that stands for really bad. Anyway, he would take over. I must admit he was pretty good on the piano but very good on the drums. Personally, I only used the piano to write songs, okay! I had my A&R job thing during the day, but at night Marvin and I would be writing songs up to midnight. Then we'd go straight to my house, where I'd have Elaine, who was my woman, fix us something to eat.

Elaine, oh yeah! She was an alluring exotic dancer, a tantalizing stripper with a body to die for. She had long, pretty legs and great calves. As you probably know by now, I'm a leg man. She had cocoa brown colored skin that helped create her stage name, "Ginger Snaps." It worked for me. The girl was hot! Elaine was a lean, mean sex machine with a temper to match!

While Marvin and I were waiting for the snacks, we'd jump on the piano at my place and finish what we were working on at the studio. It was non-stop! We both loved it. Here comes the problem. Working with Marvin, hearing him sing, play and write songs, it was obvious that he had all the ingredients that an A&R man looks for. With the gift, material, total focus, and above all the relentless pursuit to be the best, Marvin was definitely a triple threat. My job was to find the opportunity and the right song that would give Marvin the confidence to release this wealth of talent he had been given. Time was not on my side, either. You see, when the chairman wants a record on an artist, that's serious business, you feel me?

This was not helping my love life. Elaine was going crazy. She actually accused me of taking advantage of her, having her get up in the middle of the night to cook for me and whomever I happened to bring home. That's the way she put it.

"You don't live here, you live at Hitsville," she lashed out at me. "This is just a stopover. You're gonna have to make a choice between me and these all day, all night sessions. If you keep this up, one day you'll come home and I'll be gone."

I couldn't believe she'd said that! Now the girl may have had a reason or two to be upset. I knew I could be a little neglectful, even inattentive at times, but hey! Where was the love? She'd picked the wrong time to give me an ultimatum. Not when I was right on the verge of gettin' Marvin Gaye to record this R & B song we'd been working on. You feel me? I was close, real close. You see, I'd told him that we were working on a song for one of the groups, but in reality I was setting it up for him.

It was while we were writing the song Beachwood 45789 for the Marvelettes that I got my chance to convince him to record this R & B song. I gotta tell you how I did it; you're gonna love this.

I told you how we kept a tape recorder ready in every rehearsal room, by the piano, right? It was there to capture whatever lyric, melody or phrase you came up with while the idea was still in your head. You didn't wanna lose anything when you were creating, so you recorded everything right then and there. We had finally finished the last verse on the Marvelettes' song and we were ready to record the track. While we were on a roll, I suggested that we finish the other song we were working on, so we could record them both. The song just needed more lyrics for the second verse and a stronger melody in the bridge. We jumped right into it!

I began to sing the lines I'd created with more of a funky R & B flavor to them. Now in order to keep the song flowing with the same flavor, Marvin had to sing his lines the same way. Marvin liked the way I phrased my melody. He would say, "Sing that again, William R." I'd sing it again and then he would sing my melody with his words and his voice. Wow! I gotta tell you I thought I was a good R & B singer until I heard that brother! Marvin singing and phrasing the melody was fantastic, and so natural with so much feeling in it, the brother was ridiculous.

When we played the tape back on the recorder, I pointed out to Marvin how good he sounded singing R & B. Marvin would take you straight to church, make you drop some money in the basket and shout amen. Now get to this. I always knew what a great writer and producer I was, but after hearing Marvin sing, I never thought about being a recording artist again.

Anyway, I convinced him that he should record the song and I would produce it and stick with him all the way. I told him if he needed me to feed him any lines or phrases, whatever he needed, we would work it out together. He trusted me and we went into the studio and laid down tracks for Beachwood 45789 and his song, Stubborn Kind of Fellow. It was Marvin's first hit record.

Oh yeah! About Elaine, my beautiful exotic Ginger Snaps. She did it! The girl left me. This music thing got to be a little too much for her. Some of what she felt I could understand. After all, she was not getting very much attention. But I was on a roll, baby, and I thought she understood that. Man, was I mistaken.

One day out of nowhere, the woman just blew her top, with eyes all big and her face real tight. She got up in my face screaming and yellin.'

"That studio and your music is your real woman," she said. "Go make love to them and leave me alone. That's where your damn heart is! You just stop by here to change your clothes and get me to cook for you and your friends like I'm your hired help!"

She was shaking and acting crazy. "We only have sex when you feel like it." I saw a side of her I never knew existed. She had the look of a mad Black woman ready to explode! You see what I'm saying? The woman was out there. Now you just don't ignore signs like that.

Let me explain something to you, if a man or woman has the nerve to get up in your face like that, eye-to-eye and nose-to-nose, screaming and hollering about what they're not gonna take anymore, you better watch your back. Because somebody will be getting up off the floor in a minute, or wake up the next morning with some hot grits all over them. Trust me on that! Some of these sistas don't play! So to eliminate the possibility of anybody getting hurt, I thought it best to end this relationship altogether – pretty damn quick, you see what I'm sayin'? She took all her little stuff and moved out. I took care of my sons, Damian and Darrell, without any court interference, and for a while, I even took care of her, too. She came back a few years later to see if I had changed. Can you believe that? No way! This relationship was dead in the water; it was over. All we could do was remain friends. And we did, and do right up to this very day.

We followed up Marvin's hit with another hit song, Hitch Hike. Marvin would have me sit at the piano and sing the songs first, and then he would tell me to get up and shut up! He would sit down, play the piano and make the song sound like it belonged to him. That was the start of something big.

By the time we recorded his third hit single, Pride and Joy, Marvin didn't need me or anybody else to sing or phrase any song for him. He had become a master at expressing himself in the art of singing soulful songs. He was already writing them and beginning to produce them as well. I was extremely proud of him. In less than two years, Marvin Gaye had made incredible strides as a triple threat, and this was only the beginning. By the way, the song Beachwood 45789 on the Marvelettes was a hit, too.

I gotta tell you, Marvin Gaye wasn't the easiest artist to work with, mainly because of his mood swings. He could go from a stubborn kinda fellow to a sentimental softy, just like that! I guess it was part of the reason he was such a great artist. Let me give you an example of his mood swings.

Marvin and I were in my office, trying to line up his first R & B album. We were in the middle of a heated argument over what songs should go in the album. Marvin was busy trying to stick some jazz and standard songs in this R & B album, aptly called Stubborn Kind of Fellow. And I was just as busy trying to convince him that this was not the time or the album to do that. We were going at it. He was being very stubborn and I was losing the battle, when out of nowhere Andre Williams and George Gordy, one of Berry's brothers, came busting in my office with this hot idea for a song for Marvin's album. It was a song about the war.

You remember Andre Williams and Geno Parks, the two guys who sang like Sam and Dave at Denny's Show Bar, the nightclub under my old apartment? Anyway, that's the Andre who came up with this song.

The Vietnam War was going on at the time, and there was a big hit song out by the Shirelles, called Soldier Boy. This hit song was written by my man Luther Dixon and Florence Green, short for Greenberg. By the way, Florence Greenberg's life is an amazing story; when you get a chance check it out. Getting back to the song Soldier Boy, it was about a girl waiting for her soldier boy to come home.

Andre was really pumped up about this "answer song" he'd written. He wanted this song to come from the soldier's point of view. He went straight to Marvin with his dramatic pitch, tears and all, biting on his tongue and winking his eye, a nervous condition he gets whenever he's all pumped up.

"Marvin, Marvin," he said, "check this out man! I want you to picture this lonely soldier boy on the battlefield. It's raining cats and dogs, the soldier's in a foxhole with water up to here. He's looking at a picture of his girlfriend. While he's looking he begins to tear up, cry even. All the soldier can do is hope and pray that his woman, his soul mate, will still be waiting for him with open arms when he comes home." Andre raises his arms up to the sky and with tears in his eyes, he says, "I call this song A Soldier's Plea."

Andre stood there holding up his arms, biting on his tongue and winking his tear filled eyes looking at Marvin, waiting for his reaction.

Marvin looked around at everyone in the room, and with tears in his own eyes and his voice all choked up, he softly said, "A Soldier's Plea. I love it, man! I love it!" Marvin felt he could make a contribution to the soldiers in Vietnam. Needless to say, we did the song. I didn't think anything of the song, but he did. I put the song in the album along with Mr. Sandman. Hey! You gotta' give a little in order to take a little, you see what I mean?

The album was hot and Marvin Gaye was on his way. He was writing great songs with me and the other writers. Hey! Did you notice he added the letter "e" to his last name, Gay, making it Gaye! Just like his idol, Sam Cooke, who went from Cook to Cooke. Marvin wanted to be like Sam on one hand and separate himself from his father on the other. Marvin also changed Anna Gordy to Anna Gaye as they became man and wife. Like I told him, whatever works for you works for me. I ain't mad at you.

All the producers were all over Marvin with their best songs. He had material from Smokey Robinson, Holland-Dozier-Holland, Norman Whitfield, Ivy Hunter and of course William R.

He went from a crooner to the Prince of Soul. By the time he sang duets with the Ladies of Motown--Mary Wells, Kim Weston and Tammi Terrell--Marvin was crowned Prince of Motown.

STEVIE WONDERFUL

That's what Smokey Robinson calls Stevie Wonder - wonderful!

He was exactly that when he came to Motown. It all happened when Clarence Paul, one of my friends from way back, came to see me. I made mention of Clarence earlier, remember?

Clarence and I sung together as a duet; Clarence Paul and Mickey Stevenson. We were good, too. Clarence was better than I was, of course, but he was older than I was, too. The brother was tall, lighter than me and handsome. He knew more about the blues than anybody I knew. The blues was in his soul! This guy could sing it, write it, hum it, you name it, and he could do it to the blues.

When he hit those high blues notes, the girls would scream and fall out. When I took the A&R position at Motown, I brought him in to assist me and made him a producer. But Clarence had been with us for a few years and had not produced anything worth shouting about. That can be very discouraging, especially when everybody around you is producing hits. I called Clarence in for a meeting; it was time to cut the brother loose. I felt real bad about it but it had to be done. When he stepped into my office, he was all smiles.

"I'm glad you called this meeting, William R, because I wanted to talk with you, too."

"Okay, Clarence, you go first."

"No, William R., you go first!"

"Clarence, come on out with it. What's on your mind?"

When Clarence told me about this little kid he'd found sitting on some stairs, playing bongo drums, blowing a harmonica, and singing the blues, I thought maybe Clarence had had a little too much to drink for lunch. Then I remembered - he never eats lunch.

He kept raving about this kid he'd found and how he wanted to bring him to the studio and work with him. I had never seen Clarence this excited! He couldn't stop talking.

"This is the kind of artist I can work with, William R.," he said. "The kid is gonna be great! What have you got to lose? I'm gonna be the one working with him."

Clarence was rambling on and on about this kid. I had to calm the brother down.

"Relax" I said, "I'm thinking here."

I started running it over in my mind. I figured I owed Clarence for teaching me about the blues, and that it was not gonna cost me to find out if he really had something in this kid. If it didn't work out, at least I would have paid my debt to him, and I could let him go. I agreed to let him bring the kid to the studio and do his thing. That's when he laid it on me. "Oh yeah! William R., there's one other thing I forgot to tell you, man."

"Hold it, Clarence! You got the deal, my brother, don't push it."

"No, you don't understand, this is important, William R... Stevie is Blind."

I looked at Clarence like he had lost his mind. "He's what?"

"But I swear this kid can see better than people with 20/20 vision do."

All I could do was look at Clarence. He was just standing there smiling, like he knew he had me when he said "blind." I was trapped and at a loss for words. When I finally collected myself, I said, "Clarence Paul, you will be totally and completely responsible for him, you got that? In other words, you will stick with Stevie like white on rice, every minute that he's here. You got it?"

With all the stairs around this place, an accident is something I didn't even wanna think about.

"And one more thing," I said, "every time I see Stevie, I wanna see Clarence Paul. You got that?"

The smile on Clarence's face got even bigger, like he had just hit the Lotto. "I got it! I got it!"

A few days later, Clarence Paul walked in with Stevie, his mother and

116

brother, Clarence. He took Stevie into the studio and set him up on the microphone. All the producers and I came to see this wonder that Clarence had discovered. We all stood in amazement as we watched the gifts God had given to this kid. He played the bongos, the harmonica, and sang like there was no tomorrow. The rest is history.

Clarence Paul stuck with Stevie all the way. We all watched Stevie grow, learning to play every instrument in the studio. Most of them he played very well, and some of them he mastered, along with mastering the arts of songwriting and producing. God gave him the gifts, and Stevie was relentless in developing them. Clarence Paul got his mega hit with Fingertips, Motown gained a legendary superstar, and God gave us another witness to how great Thou art.

Things were going great. I was busy working with as many people as I could. I had teamed up with Barrett Strong for Eddie Holland's Jamie, and with Marvin for the Marvelettes' "Beachwood 45789."

B.G. had his hit record on Marvin Gaye's Stubborn Kind of Fellow, with Martha Reeves and her group the Vandellas singing background. Now that was some good stuff goin' on.

And the hits just kept on coming.

YOU BEAT ME TO THE PUNCH

I had just finished producing the hit record, Jamie, on Eddie Holland. Eddie sounded just like Jackie Wilson, and he was as good looking as Jackie, too, maybe even better because he was younger. I worked on Eddie's act personally. I was getting him ready to go on the road. I felt he was gonna be the next Jackie Wilson. With me and the Motown machine behind him, it was a win-win situation. We were getting another Motown review ready to go out with the Supremes, who were hot, hot, hot! And this time, they didn't have to ask me to go, I was ready, and Eddie Holland was going with us. I had it all planned out.

Now picture this; I got Eddie dressed in this great-looking all white outfit, right down to the shoes, baby. The brother looked like a walking angel. He had the girls backstage eating out of his hand. I had placed Eddie right in the sweet spot of the show. Right after Mary Wells' song, You Beat Me to the Punch Eddie would step out on stage and give the girls in the audience that big smile of his. As the girls screamed and hollered, that's when I would start the intro.

With me conducting the band on my own hit song, I could just feel this was going to be the show's coup de grâce. Eddie was all nerves waiting in the wings as they announced Mary Wells. As Mary stepped on the stage, I kicked off the intro to her opening song. Out of nowhere, Herman Griffin (Mary's husband) appeared dressed in an all-white tuxedo with tails. His hair was slicked back, and he was wearing way too much make-up, which was the wrong color. He was dancing and smiling at the audience, shaking his head and waving a baton in his hand. He looked like a bad version of Cab Calloway.

He danced over to me, wiggling like a snake and said, "I'm conducting the show for my wife. You got a problem with that?"

Before I could say anything, he jumped in front of the band and started conducting the orchestra. He never stopped wiggling and waving that damn baton. I gave him the high five as I walked off the stage, acting like it was all part of the show. Herman was grinning like the cat that just swallowed the canary.

119

All I could do was smile back at him. That son of a gun stole my idea and upstaged Eddie Holland with the white suit bit, I thought. Man was I pissed off, and there was nothing I could do but grin and bear it. It gets better. Get to this!

While Mary Wells was singing her heart out, Herman was behind her conducting the band and the audience loved it. Right at the point when she started singing, You Beat Me to the Punch, Herman all of a sudden did a triple back flip, Bam! Bam! Bam! The audience went crazy, laughing and shouting.

Mary couldn't understand why the audience was laughing, what was going on. When she looked back at Herman, he was as cool as can be, conducting the band with a smile on his face like nothing had happened. Mary, confused, turned back to the audience as she continued to sing her heart out. When she reached the punch line again, out of nowhere, Bam! Bam! Bam! Herman did it again, another triple back flip. The audience went wild, laughing and shouting even harder.

Mary ended the song and ran off the stage crying, while Herman was busy taking two and three bows. The audience was laughing and applauding him as if he were the star. Herman was eating it up. He called me back onstage and calmly handed me the baton. With a big grin of satisfaction all over his face, he turned to the audience and took another bow, then walked off with a swagger, leaving the audience in a frenzy! I knew we were going to have trouble with this brother. Herman had plans for himself and his wife Mary Wells, and they did not include Motown.

It was Eddie Holland's turn onstage. Eddie was already as nervous as he could be and now he had to follow that madness. I immediately started the intro to Eddie's hit song, Jamie. Eddie nervously walked out onstage in his white suit, which was not as effective at all, thanks to Herman "Cab Calloway" Griffin, doing triple back over flips in his white tails.

Eddie walked up to the microphone and just stood there. After letting the intro to his song go by twice, I figured he was way too nervous. I started the intro once again, and Eddie just stood there looking lost. While I was conducting the band, I worked my way over to him and said, "Sing, man, sing."

He jumped right into the song. The beginning was terrible. You could hear how nervous he was throughout the song. He finally got control of it toward the end; better late than never. We were all glad when it was over, including Eddie. Smokey Robinson and the Miracles came on right behind Eddie, singing Shop Around, to save the day.

That was my last trip with the Motown Review and Eddie Holland's last stage performance for me.

The Motown Review went out again. But for the most part, it was over. We sold a lot of records while the review was out, but the artists started making more money working their own shows. The Motown Review had served its purpose.

MR. ROBINSON

Let's talk about the unique and exceptionally gifted Smokey Robinson; singer, writer, producer, entertainer, and my brother from another mother. Smokey couldn't stop singing, writing and producing even if he'd wanted to. He wrote on the road, in the car, on newspaper, in the bathroom on toilet paper, on a napkin in the bar, in the bed, on his head, no! no! I just threw the "on his head" thing in there to see if you were paying attention.

All kidding aside, after meeting Smokey I wondered why the chairman didn't pick him to be the A&R man. Smokey and the Miracles were obviously an integral part of Berry's plan. Smokey was already working with B.G., writing and producing, when I joined the company. He knew all about my work with the Hamptones, singing jazz on the road and everything. He and I hit it off immediately. He even asked me if I would teach him and the Miracles some jazz songs. I wondered why they wanted to learn jazz; they were doing all right singing what they were singing. I told him I'd be glad to teach them, and I did.

We started playing golf together, hung out at the clubs and everything - everything except the after-hours joints. Smokey would not go to any of the after-hours joints with me; that was a no-no! He had a thing about after-hours joints. The drinking, the gambling, the chance of getting busted and going to jail overnight did not appeal to Smokey.

As I watched him write his wonderful romantic songs and as I listened to the lyrics, I became acutely aware that it required a tenderhearted person, one with a romantic nature, to write such touching songs of love. The A&R man position required just the opposite. Not that I don't have a tender heart, mind you, but I'm the first to admit it's nowhere near as tender as Smokey Robinson's, and that's the truth!

As for having a romantic nature working with artists and musicians? That's a joke! Now having a compromising nature? Yes! Even an understanding nature works, but a romantic one, forget about it! The artists and the musicians will wear your ass out!

Berry Gordy found true magic in Smokey Robinson. Smokey delivered the goods again and again, with his million-seller Shop Around and You Really Got a Hold On Me and my favorite, Tracks Of My Tears.

Even the Beatles, among other artists who loved the Motown sound, jumped all over some Smokey Robinson songs. Who could resist lyrics like; I don't like you, but I love you, Seems that I'm always thinking of you.

Now is the brother out there or what? No wonder the hits kept on coming. I gotta give it to B.G., he knew exactly what he was doing when he picked me for the A&R man and let Smokey Robinson write and produce his wonderful songs.

And the hits just kept on coming.

ADVENTURES IN A&R LAND

Motown was selling records and my override money (my royalty from Motown records, regardless of who had produced them) was growing. The Supremes were on fire. All the girl groups were charting, hot and heavy. The Marvelettes, The Velvelettes, Martha and The Vandellas, even Kim Weston had a hit goin.' I was thinking I had everything under control and going smooth.

That little bubble of euphoria was a joke!

To start with, Martha Reeves was getting jealous of all the attention being given to the Supremes. I'm sure some of the other girls were feeling it, too, but they lacked the heart to voice their feelings. Not my girl Martha. She let it be known that she was not happy about it one bit! When it comes to artists being jealous of one another, especially females, you can forget about it! You see, trying to appease them is out of the question.

Hey! It gets worse.

In the midst of this entire feline jealousy, I get a call from the chairman about Mary Wells. The promotion department wanted Mary's record, and they wanted it now! When they said now, they meant like yesterday! She was supposed to be in the studio working on it, but the girl was having problems with Herman, that husband of hers. You remember him at the Apollo Theater? The one in the white suit doing back over flips Bam! Bam! Bam!

I told B.G. I would get on it right away. I called Herman to tell him we needed Mary in the studio ASAP. Before I could finish talking, Herman hung up on me! Now, I know he's not that crazy! So I called right back. This time someone picked up the phone but wouldn't say anything. I kept saying, "Hello! Hello!"

All of a sudden I heard Mary crying and screaming in the background, "Help! Help! He won't let me out of here!"

I jumped in the car with my two boys and went straight over to her house. Now we all know how Herman felt about me. So I thought I'd better be prepared for any foolish moves that the brother might make. I took a golf club from the trunk of my car, just in case.

When I knocked on the door, I could hear Herman cursing and screaming like a drunken sailor. "Who is it? And what the hell do you want?" He opened the door, saw me standing there with the nine-iron in my hand and started apologizing.

"Hey! Mickey, I didn't know it was you, man. Somebody's been calling on the phone and hanging up on me, knocking on my door and then running away, man. I thought it was them comin' back. Come on in, Mickey, I was just talking to Mary about going down to the studio and finishing that album she's been working on." He looked at Mary. "Wasn't I, baby?"

Mary looked scared and confused. "Yeah that's right," she said.

"That's good Herman," I said, "because the producers and the musicians are all in the studio waiting for your baby! So I know you won't mind if I take her back to the studio with me. You got a problem with that?" Before Herman could answer, I told my two boys to escort Mary to the car.

Herman followed us, apologizing, telling me that he wasn't trying to keep Mary from the studio. "I know she has to record, man, I ain't that crazy. Mary, baby, I'll be down there later, baby."

As we drove off, Mary tried to convince me that Herman didn't mean any harm. She said he was just trying to do the right thing. "He's my manager now, Mickey. I know he loves me and he's gonna look out for my best interests." She talked all the way to the studio; I don't know whether she was trying to convince me or herself that she did the right thing by putting Herman in charge of her career.

Mary had a string of hits, and Smokey Robinson's song My Guy took her over the top. Now that Herman was her manager and husband, I knew we hadn't heard the last of Herman Griffin, not by a long shot. Herman pulled every trick he could think of to keep Mary from recording; leaving town, missing dates, pretending to be sick, and more. It wasn't long before Herman and Mary walked into B.G.'s office wanting a release from Motown. Herman even alluded to a law suit protesting the signing of Mary's original contracts, claiming she was only seventeen at the time she signed. He wanted to take her to another label where he could also be her manager and producer.

After Herman's harassment and insistence on pulling his wife off the label, B.G. finally gave Mary Wells her release from Motown, along with a fair settlement. Personally, I was surprised and I'll tell you why.

There was an unwritten law at Motown. Once we signed an artist to the label, it was for the length of the contract. If artists chose to extend their contracts, it was because the finances, marketing, promotion and material had proven to be promising and outstanding. Now if they wanted to stay with Motown Records, it was because all the above obligations had been met, above and beyond expectation.

But the feeling of being a part of the most spontaneous and innovative record company of its time, one that was making history all over the world, was a feeling of euphoria. I truly believed it to be a gift from God! Ninety-eight percent of the artists re-signed their contracts with Motown because they wanted! I repeat wanted to stay, and they did.

Berry would express his personal feelings about artists who signed with us. To him, it was more than a commitment. When you joined the Motown family, you were now under the covenant, which meant Motown was obligated to do all that we could do for the artists and their careers.

That's one of the reasons we had the studio lights burning day and night, producers and writers working 'round the clock, and the artist development classes going on all day long. We wanted to level the playing field so that every Motown artist had more than a chance. They needed a fighting chance. And there is a difference. You know what I mean?

I want you to know that Berry Gordy, Jr., never really fired anybody. He would find a way to keep everybody around. The chairman was very sympathetic toward the people at Motown and would find them another position in the company before he'd let them go. Most of them would end up in my department, so I had to find something for them to do. I would keep them around for a while, but I was not like B.G. If they couldn't cut it, they were history.

I believe Berry Gordy, Jr., and Smokey Robinson have the same kinda hearts. Like my grandmother used to say, "He got a heart as soft as I don't know what," and that's my personal opinion.

Some of the artists thought B.G. had a magic touch or something. Wrong! It was my ass, along with the writers and producers coming up with the hits that made his magic work. Some of the artists looked at Berry

Gordy, Jr., as some kinda genius. I won't argue that point with you. To each his own. I will say this; one of the gifts bestowed on Berry was the ability to choose the right people at the right time, to do great things. His aptness and specialty was in the gift of motivating and inspiring his people to stretch their imaginations and come up with great products and ideas. He pushed us all to the limit. B.G. would say, "That's good! But I think you can do better," and they all did better, including me, over and over again.

Let's get back to Mary Wells and her husband, Herman. His plan was to take Mary to 20th Century Fox Records, where he had cut a deal for her in advance. That's the reason he was going through all that mess; he had to deliver her. What Herman didn't know was that Mary Wells was a difficult artist to record.

She had this raspy voice that B.G. fell in love with when he first heard her sing "Bye Bye Baby" and he signed her on the spot. I never would have signed her, which goes to show you I don't know everything. Herman never knew about the difficulty in recording Mary Wells, because as A&R director, I had a standing rule. I would not allow anyone in the studio, not friends, family, husbands or lovers, nobody but the producers, the writers, and the artists. This was the only way that the producers had the freedom to correct artists without embarrassing them or putting them on the defensive. In other words, the artist could take constructive criticism without having to save face in front of an audience.

With Mary, it took considerable overdubbing to get the best sound out of her voice. The producers who worked with her were the keys to her success. Producers like Smokey Robinson, Clarence Paul, Holland-Dozier-Holland, even me, we all knew how to produce and record Mary Wells. After Herman had a few failures as her producer, 20th Century discovered that it was the Motown producers who gave Mary her hits.

They called me to ask if I would come over to 20th Century and produce an album on Mary Wells. They offered me a lot of money. Not only did I turn them down, but I called a meeting of all the producers and writers, and I told them that under no circumstance could any of them produce or write anything on Mary Wells. I wanted to be informed about any and all contact made by 20th Century or anyone else concerning Mary Wells. By the way, nobody made a move toward Mary or that record company.

And the hits just kept on coming.

FAMILY NOTES

Just to bring you up to date, let's talk about my biological brothers and my sister.

My baby brother Martin went off to join the Army, and they made him an M.P. Big mistake! That was like turning a pit bull loose in a pet store. My little brother Martin was about five feet five. He had grown up with a very serious Napoleon complex, which got worse as he grew older. The Army knew what they were doing by making Martin an M.P. The Army was a melting pot of men from all different backgrounds and temperaments; combine that with unchecked coping mechanisms, vices, alcohol, drugs, depression and mental trauma you've got walking grenades with no pins that had to be caught, controlled and brought back in. Martin would attack a guy six feet tall like he was a midget. He would walk right up to a soldier who was AWOL (absent without leave) or something, and without warning, whack him upside the head with his billy-club, hard and fast, knocking the poor guy out cold! While he was unconscious, Martin would put the handcuffs on him and drag him to the jeep while reading the soldier his rights. Martin would always get his man.

My brother Lonnie, on the other hand, wanted to be an actor/director. So when I started making money, I sent him to New York to study at the Berkoff School of the Arts. In the Sixties and Seventies it was the best school in New York. I rented an apartment in the Village for him with all the trimmings, furniture, clothes, and food, you name it. I gave my brother Lonnie everything but a car, which was not a smart buy in the Big Apple unless you had a place to park it. Putting my brother in school really paid off for him and me. Lonnie became a good acting coach and director. He directed one of my shows which won three awards.

I was so into my brothers, I forgot about my sister, Elaine. I did mention her, didn't I? If I didn't dwell on her it's because my sister Elaine was not into show business at all. She liked music, but Elaine couldn't sing or dance a lick. With all this talent in the family, somehow my sister got passed over completely. She got married early and had three kids, two girls and a boy. And they were just like their mother; they couldn't sing or dance, either. Now tell me God doesn't have a sense of humor?

Moving right along, I had two sons by my first wife, Betty Ann. That marriage ended in a bitter divorce. It was so bitter that it's in the law books in Michigan, under Stevenson versus Stevenson.

Between her mother telling her how to live and her father, a "jackleg" preacher who popped in and out of her life whenever he felt like it, my wife Betty did not enjoy the benefits of a father/daughter relationship. I have no idea what that preacher did to her mother, but after he left – she never married or even thought of getting married again. All I know is her influence over her daughter was too much for me; like mother like daughter. I had to get out of there.

All of these things contributed to Betty Ann's insecure and confused way of dealing with me.

You know what they say; Like mother like daughter, like father like son.

THE ATLANTIC CITY
MOTOWN CONNECTION

In the '60s and early '70s, the boardwalk in Atlantic City was the place for artists to work. This was before the big casinos moved in. It was the hottest spot for Black entertainment on the east coast. There were nightclubs all over the place. The big clubs would hold over a thousand people, and the small ones would hold 700 or more. Even the smaller ones would hold two or three hundred.

Atlantic City stayed open around the clock, and when the clubs closed to clean up, the bars would stay open until the clubs opened up again - it never stopped. None of the clubs had any décor or ambience to speak of. They were just huge buildings, each with a stage and a long liquor bar like in the old western salons. Some even had sawdust on the floors, but all of them had lots of people inside.

People could be seen drinking and having big fun, dancing and swinging to great music, being entertained by the best R & B singers, jazz artists, big bands, small bands, comics, and production shows of all kinds. You name it Atlantic City had it goin' on. If an act was good, it performed from 8 p.m. until 2 a.m., prime time in Atlantic City. The bad acts would only come on at four in the morning, when everybody was either out cold or too drunk to know the difference. Atlantic City was where Black artists could do their thing, baby!

It was a smorgasbord of live entertainment, a carnival around the clock, twenty-four seven! The public loved it, Blacks, whites, young, and old, they could see everybody from Aretha Franklin to Count Basie, from Marvin Gaye to Ike and Tina Turner, with James Brown and B.B. King, Nancy Wilson, Etta James, Kim Weston, and the Temptations thrown in for kicks. At any given time, Motown would have three or four artists performing in Atlantic City.

It was in Atlantic City that I met Lon Fontaine and Gil Askey, two of the most talented people I've ever had the good fortune to meet. Motown was fortunate enough to have them become part of the family.

This is the way it went down. We had two acts performing in the city at the same time, The Temptations and The Four Tops. I was busy club

131

hopping, checking and fixing things with both acts. On this particular night, I decided to give myself a break, you know, find a hot date or something. I walked into one of the nicest night clubs in Atlantic City. This club was hot! It had the look and the feel of a classic night club. The tables were covered with red cloths, and each table had a small lamp on it that gave off just enough light to read the menu. They had nice soft plush chairs that matched the room's colorful décor. The lighting and the atmosphere were the kind that put you in a relaxed mood, and I needed that. The waitresses looked good too baby. All of them had legs for days (that means long and pretty, okay?)

I was there to see a production called The Larry Steel Smart Affairs. I was told that this production had ten of the most beautiful Black women in the world, dancing in the show. And they were right! Not only were they beautiful, but they could all dance their asses off, and they had some nice asses too, oops! Sorry 'bout that! The choreography was fantastic, and the costumes were skimpy, colorful, and unique.

They made the movements of the girls look even more alluring. The music was the bomb! A fusion of jazz and funk set to a big band arrangement, I loved every minute of it. I wanted to meet the people who made it happen. All I could think of was that we had to have that kind of talent and production value at our fingertips at Motown. This was the future, and I wanted us to be ready for it. I didn't know how I was gonna pull it off, but I was going after it, so I went to work.

I invited the conductor and the choreographer to my table for a drink, one at a time. First I got choreographer Lon Fontaine. He came with five of his dancers. They were all excited to meet the man from Motown Records, but not half as excited as I was to meet them. You see, I was trying to figure out which one of these fine brown frames was gonna spend the rest of the evening with me. I bought champagne for Lon and Long Island iced teas for all the girls. I'll let you in on a little secret. Two glasses of that Long Island iced tea makes you say, "Let's party!" After a couple of drinks, I found out from the girls that Lon created the costumes to go with the dance. The girls loved Motown, the artists, the music, everything. They were true fans. The artists they loved most of all were The Temptations. The girls started talking about how hot The Temptations' songs were and which one they liked the most and how they'd like to meet them, all that girly stuff. "They are five fine, long, tall lanky looking men, too," said Lon. One of the girls jumped out of her chair, snapped her fingers, shook her hips and said, "I know that's right, baby."

Lon and the other girls broke out laughing and high five-ing each other. I think the booze was getting to them; it gave me a chance to zero in on the girl I wanted.

Okay! I told the girls I'd introduce them to The Temptations personally. The dancers started helping me convince Lon that Motown was where he should be. I assured Lon that he would have a whole stable of talented artists to work with, including The Temptations. And whatever he was making here, I would double it! That did it, Lon was in. I had Lon introduce me to Gil Askey, the arranger and conductor of all that wonderful music in the show. Gil sat down at my table, folded his arms and began to look me over. Now, that took me by surprise. I had no idea what Lon had told him about me or what he was thinking. He just sat there looking at me. I decided to break the silence and introduce myself.

That's when he opened up the conversation with a stutter. "S-s-s-so you're the m-m-m-man from m-m-m--"

I jumped in and said, "Motown. I'm Mickey Stevenson. I'm the A&R man."

I reached out to shake his hand, when he asked me, "W-w-w-w-what d-d-d- do you d-d-d-do (he took a breath) as the a-a-a-a-a---"

I jumped in again. "As the A&R man, I put the artists and talented people like you together, to make great music, like the music you did in this show."

I knew I was in for a long talk, so I decided to cut to the chase. "Gil, can I call you Gil? We have a stable of young talented artists who could use your gift of music. They need it now, while they're young enough to absorb it. This way it can stay with them throughout their careers."

I could tell he was a bit apprehensive. His musical background was obviously based in jazz, but I kept talking, and after a few drinks or more I got him to see that jazz, blues, and R & B were all the same music. Most of it comes from the same source, if you wanna know the truth: "gospel music," at least for Black folks.

"Ttthe yyyyoung pepeppeople ttthat I ssssee, they dddon't wwwwant to lllllisten to no bbody. I gggot that pprobblem right here."

When Gil stopped to take a breath, I jumped in again. "It's about what's in your heart, Gil. That's what makes the difference, right?"

While he was nodding his head in agreement, I said, "After the music I just heard, man, for you to blend all the wonderful sounds and rhythms in your head with the music of Motown that would be awesome. We could all learn something from you, my brother. Gil Askey, you're the man!"

I could see he was thinking about it. "Sssshowing ttthe young ppppeople sssomething about rrreal mmmmusic, (he took a long breath) nnnnnow that wwwwould be an aaaaccom pppp--"

I couldn't wait for this word so I jumped in. "Accomplishment." I added, "And to top it off, you will be well paid. Motown is like no other record company in the business. We're on a mission!"

Gil gave me a strange look. "Mmmickey Ssstevenson, yyou really gggot a ppppassion fffor this cccompany, and I llllike that."

Before I left Atlantic City, both Gil Askey and Lon Fontaine were committed to join the Motown family. Oh! I forgot to mention, the Long Island iced tea thing, you know the drinks I got for the girls, well, it worked like a charm! One of the dancers and I messed around and fell in love for three days.

Gil Askey had to be in New York at the Apollo with the house band for three weeks, and when I called him on the backstage phone at the Apollo, he was surprised. I told him his airline ticket was at the airport, and a car would be picking him up when he arrived in Detroit.

All Gil could say was "Mmmmickey Ssssstevenssson, you ssssomething else, I'll bbbbbe there."

When Lon Fontaine and Gil Askey arrived in Detroit, I gotta tell ya, I was quite proud of that. B.G. called me into his office to talk about a memo from the finance department.

"What is this? Who are these two people you wanna just add to the payroll?"

I started to explain who they were when he cut me off, " If they don't work out, this money will be coming out of your pocket," he warned.

"And if they do work out, do I get a raise?"

He looked at me, familiar grin in place. "No! That's what you're here for, that's your job. You're the A&R man, remember?" He walked away, smiling.

I was smiling, too. You see, for me to hire an arranger is one thing, but to hire a choreographer, that's crossing the line a bit. Berry knew my passion for Motown, and he trusted me.

Lon Fontaine went to work right away teaching the artists choreography to enhance their songs and stage performances. The rehearsal studio was across the street from the recording studio. Each artist had to do a two hour session with Lon Fontaine, three days a week. Lon wasn't just a choreographer, the man was a perfectionist. He would work you to death going over the hand movements, the fingers, and how the legs should look when you stopped dancing. He was absolutely devoted to perfectionism.

In the beginning, some of the artists would cut their rehearsal time with Lon as short as they could, using all kind of excuses, from "my mother is sick" to "I have to go to the bathroom" and never come back. Some of the artists were not ready to accept the idea of being groomed. They felt that what they were doing onstage was good enough, and they had no intention of doing any more than they had to do.

Now the artists who recognized choreography and grooming as an opportunity to become more dynamic onstage, like The Four Tops and The Tempting Temptations, they were the ones who went at it with a passion. It was Lon who came up with the idea of building a mic stand with five mics on it for The Temptations. It was great! It made their choreography look so dramatic.

When the chairman found out what Lon was capable of doing with the artists, he wasted no time putting The Supremes with Lon.

They had a number one record, and the chairman wanted a number one act.

DIANA ROSS

This is a good spot to shine the light on another Motown artist who became a superstar; Diana Ross. Not the Dream Girls' version, which Beyoncé played in a stunningly complimentary performance. I'm talking about the real Diana Ross, the one who came out of the projects of Detroit. The real Diana, who had one of the leanest bodies I'd ever seen, with her short hair, and her big pretty eyes. She had the heart of a lion and the focus of an eagle.

I never really knew how she felt about me or if she had any feeling at all about me. I do know that she always gave me respect. To be quite honest with you, that's all you can ask of the people who work with you. She was one of the main artists choreographed by Lon Fountain, she and the Supremes.

When Lon Fountain met Diana Ross he met his match. She could take everything he dished out and more. Diana saw what this could do for her career, and she was on it. She made up her mind to learn all she could from Lon and went at it tooth and nail. She loved learning, and Lon loved teaching her, plus she looked good doing it.

Now Miss Ross would stay overtime, I mean way overtime. She and Lon would do the routines over and over again until she got them right. I admired her tenacity and work habits. She stayed focused while she worked through the entire routine, from the choreography to the dialogue, right into the songs. Lon would say, "Get it right! Now do it again! What can you do that will make it better? Now what can you do to make it yours?" Sometimes the rehearsals would start off with three Supremes, but end up with only one, Diana, and she would be in there working her butt off. The girl was relentless, and it was obvious that she would become a star. She wanted to be the best. I saw it, Lon saw it, the producers saw it, and Berry Gordy knew it. She went from the Supremes to Diana Ross and the Supremes.

That next step was predictable. It couldn't go any other way. Smokey Robinson went from the Miracles to Smokey Robinson and the Miracles. That step was predictable as well. As for the chairman breaking up groups and throwing people out as rumored, that's bullshit. Let me break it down for you.

When an artist in a group, for example, a band or singers, makes up his mind that he wants to go it alone, the record company has two choices - you either help the artist achieve what he's after, or you release him and let him sign with some other record company that understands his ambitious desire, and will allow them to do his own thing. The latter would be stupid, don't you think?

Historical movements of lead singers in groups will bear this out. Eighty-five percent of the groups that start out together, Black or White, eventually have a lead singer or some member of the group announce, "I'm outta here! I gotta do my own thing." From the Beatles to the Black Eyed Peas, from N'Sync's Justin Timberlake, and all the groups in between. Ask Beyoncé, who started with her group, Destiny's Child. Okay! She'll tell you what I'm talking about.

Diana Ross made the world pay attention to her, and I ain't mad at her! Neither was the chairman, as we all watched her develop into one of the finest entertainers in the world. I mean fine as in beautiful, sexy, with a whole lotta class, baby. I could do thirty pages on Diana Ross and the Supremes, but you can read all about them in Diana's book, and if you wanna get personal, read Mary Wilson's book.

The artists who didn't believe in perfecting their showmanship saw the differences in the ones who worked at it. It wasn't long before everybody wanted their rehearsal time with Lon Fontaine. We got so busy we had to bring on Charlie Atkins, another choreographer, Maurice King, an arranger/conductor, Miss Powell, who would groom the girls in make-up, how to sit, walk, and talk; the whole nine yards. Together they inspired a renewed self-confidence to the artist and production value to their performances.

It all helped make the Motown artists unique. Their live performances on stage and television set such a precedent that, for years, artists all over the world imitated them. Other artists copied their arrangements, routines, style, and movements, from The Temptations' Ain't Too Proud to Beg dance steps to The Supremes' hand movements in Stop In The Name Of Love and even to the Four Tops' rockin' Sugar Pie Honey Bunch. I would venture to say that it all worked out like a charm. Gil Askey started working on the musical arrangements, taking the artists to a new level. He made The Four Tops' music sound fantastic onstage.

When B.G. saw how incredible Gil was, he immediately assigned him to his number one act as well, The Supremes, and finally to Diana Ross.

He stayed with Diana as her arranger and conductor forever. Gil Askey had that magic touch.

Right here I'd like to jump ahead a bit to the year 2006, at Janie Bradford's yearly HAL (Heroes and Legends) awards in Los Angeles. Gil Askey received the honorary HAL award for his contributions during 40 years in show business. Gil received an overwhelming, standing ovation that brought tears to his eyes.

When the ovation settled down and everyone took their seats, Gil Askey looked at me from the podium with his tear filled eyes and said, "The mmmeeting that I had in Atlantic City with you, MMickey Stevenson, it changed my life, and I just wanna say tthank you, Mmmickey, thank you."

I gotta tell you it brought tears to my eyes, too.

Then he turned to the chairman and said,

" Ttthank you, Bbberry Gordy, for lllletting me bbbe a part of the mm Motown family all these years. The trip was gg grea--fantastic!"

Now let's get back to the A&R man.

RAINBOWS AND RIOTS

If you were a producer working at Motown, you always got to the studio early, and you shouldn't have been surprised if, when you got there, you saw four or five other producers and writers already waiting in line for studio time. This creative process was being duplicated by all the producers; Holland-Dozier-Holland, Smokey, Marvin Gaye, Harvey, Stevie Wonderful and Norman Whitfield. You gotta understand - we all loved it. What looked like work to others was a labor of love to us. It was great.

Motown was taking a giant stride. We bought another building to house our own sales and promotions department; this we needed badly. I'm not talking about the building; I'm talking about our own sales and promotion staff. Look! We were selling records all right, but the independent promotion guys we had to hire were costing us a fortune. Not to mention the other gifts and goodies we were constantly supplying. You know what I mean? The DJ's and program directors were all demanding a lot of expensive gifts. They wanted it all just to put our records on the radio. And I'm talking about the Black stations, too. All the other record companies were giving it up, so we were forced to comply as well.

Collecting a dollar from the independent distributors and the one stops that carried the Motown line was like pulling teeth. They would sell our records and hold our money, then tell us they didn't collect it from their accounts. You're gonna love this one. The accounts they were talking about were the mama and papa stores in the Black neighborhoods. These were the same mama and papa stores that most distributors, wouldn't dare give credit to in the first place, not without having them sign away their life savings. The situation was getting out of hand.

Let's back up a minute. Let me explain something to those of you who don't understand what I'm talking about when I say "independent distributors" and "one stops." Let's call them "Indies" for short.

The role the Indies played with Motown and other independent record companies went like this; From 1955 to 1985, before the big major record companies started buying up the small but successful independent record companies (such as A & M Records, Atlantic, ATCO Records, Philly International Records, Stax Records, Roulette, Fantasy, and King Records, including ninety percent of all the gospel labels, along with Motown Records), everyone had to go through independent distributors and one stops (smaller outlets) in order to sell their product. The Indies were the only way you got your records to the marketplace; outlets like retail stores, record shops, even all the neighborhood mama and papa shops.

Major companies--CBS, RCA, MGM, ABC, MCA, and Capitol Records, for example--didn't have this problem, but all the independent record companies did. Since the Indies had a monopoly on the retail outlets, they paid us when they wanted to and how they wanted to. Some didn't pay at all. There wasn't much any of us could do about it. We had to beg, plead, or sue to get our money. If you were a Black company, you could forget about two of those options, if you know what I mean!

Motown had so many hits out and more product coming. Hey! We were a cash cow. So it behooved the Indies to pay us just enough of our money to keep us on the hook, you see what I mean? For the independent distributors and one-stops, trying to keep most of our money was the new game in town. I remember B.G. giving me my override check for all the records sold in the last six months. The check looked very small. When he handed it to me, I said, "Hey! What is this? I thought we were selling records!"

"We are," he said, "but it's getting harder and harder to collect our money from the distributors. They're not sending in the payments and they're coming up with excuses. You know the old 'checks are in the mail' trick. But don't worry. I'm bringing in someone to fix it."

That's when the company met Barney Ales. The words "to fix it" were an understatement.

What B.G. should've said was he was bringing in "the fixer." Barney was a big, strong, mean machine. He must have weighed over two hundred and fifty pounds, packed with muscle, in more ways than one. A tall man, he could carry the weight very well. He had salt and pepper hair that matched his well-trimmed beard. All the females, including the artists at the company, thought Barney was very handsome. Some said he favored Kenny Rogers. As far as I was concerned, he wasn't all that! He looked all right for a white boy. Hey! Barney, I was just kidding; in case you're reading this, you were my main man.

Barney and I became very good friends from day one. You see, he was from the streets, and he didn't play around about money or anything else for that matter. The first thing he did after putting his promotion staff together was to send them out in pairs, to collect some of the money owed to us by the distributors. I went along to Chicago with Ira, one of the new promotion guys. We stayed in a motel on the south side of Chicago.

Now, imagine this; Ira a very clean-cut, sophisticated Jewish fella, the kind who's into brushing his teeth and combing his hair before he put his pajamas on. Then he'd climb into his nice warm beddy-bye and off to sleep he'd go. A young Jewish guy stuck in a motel on the south side of Chicago in the '60s, with a Black man for a roommate who sleeps in his shorts with one hand on his gun under the pillow, and the other hand on the TV remote, changing channels all night long.

Now picture this; there was only one bed in the room for the two of us, and it was not, and I repeat not, a king-sized bed. As a matter of fact, it was kinda small, just big enough for a person and a half. It was late when we landed in Chicago, so the moment we checked into the room, I started taking off my clothes to get ready for bed. I took my gun and stuck it under my pillow and started my TV bit.

You know how we like to change the channels, trying to find something at that hour to put us to sleep. In those days, you didn't have many channels to choose from. While I'm flipping through the TV looking for something, anything to watch, Ira just sat on the side of the bed, kinda frozen.

I asked him, "What in the hell's the matter with you?"

He looked at me all scared and said, "What is the gun for?"

"Do you really wanna know? I'll tell ya, it's very simple, Ira. You got this Black guy--me--and this white boy--you--sleeping together in a cheap motel on the south side of Chicago. Now some of the people in this fine establishment may find something wrong with this picture. Okay? They may even try to investigate. So this little .38 Special right here, will make a sucker think twice, you see what I mean? And tomorrow, we're gonna be in the wrong place at the wrong time again, hopefully to pick up some cash. I'm not about to get my ass jacked up by some junky."

I think my answer might have made things worse, I don't know. What I do know is I was done with that conversation, so I got under the covers and went back to flipping channels on the TV. Ira finally got his nerves together and did the strangest thing.

He took his pajamas, went into the bathroom, turned off the lights and changed into his PJ's in the dark. Then he ran out of the bathroom like a bat out of hell and jumped in the bed. He was so far over on the edge of that small bed, I thought he was gonna fall on the floor.

After I finished laughing my ass off, I told him, "Don't worry. I'm not interested in you; you ain't that cute! I'm more concerned about the people I hear walking up and down the hallway outside this door. But never fear," I said, waving my gun around, "I got your back. This will take care of both of us, okay? So you can carry your little pale, narrow ass to sleep."

The next day we went to the distributors. The front of the building had a large glass window. When you looked in, you could see a spiral staircase, and at the top some guy was sitting at a desk. When I pushed the intercom, we heard him ask, "Who is it?"

I said, "It's Mickey Stevenson, from Motown Records. We've come to collect our money."

His voice got real loud. "We're not open today. Anyway, your check's in the mail."

I got even louder. "Why don't you cancel that check, man, and just give us the cash?"

In reply, a big Great Dane came running up to the door, growling and showing its teeth. You could tell it was one of those trained dogs, the kind the police use during riots. Ira was ready to run, and I couldn't blame him. That dog looked vicious.

The voice over the intercom said, "Get away from that door."

Okay! That's it! After putting up with Ira acting crazy, people walking up and down the hall in the hotel all night, and now this Great Dane looking at me like I'm lunch, I was pissed. I pushed the intercom button, pulled out my .38 and said, "If you don't open this damn door and call off that stupid-looking dog, I'm gonna shoot him right through the damn glass and then I'm coming up there and pay you a visit, okay?"

The man blew some kind of whistle and the dog moved away. Opening the door, he said, "I was only kidding, come on in."

We got most of our money without too much trouble and took a flight back to Detroit that evening.

We could've left earlier, but there was the matter of a soul food restaurant near the Regal Theater that also needed my attention.

I had to have some of their smothered pork chops, with rice and gravy and those hot buttered biscuits that melted in your mouth. Oh yeah, and a side order of candied yams, baby. I took Ira there so he could taste some real deal soul food for the first time. He had a ball.

If a distributor or one-stop didn't pay us, Barney would threaten to remove the Motown product. Most of them started paying. As for the ones who couldn't pay fast enough, Barney did exactly what he said he would do. The next day the trucks would roll up to that Indie's place of business, some guys would jump out and start loading all the Motown stock out of their place. They'd take it to another distributor, right next door if need be. When the news got around that you could lose the Motown line, the cash cow, the other Indies started to come up with that money, baby!

Like I said, Barney was the vice-president in charge of sales, promotion, and, in my opinion, collections. Barney Ales put together a promotion staff you would not believe. It consisted of an Arab, a Jew, a Black man and some Caucasians. They were Mel De Curb, Irving Beagle, Larry Maxwell, Gil Bourges, Phil Jones, Russ Reagan (our man on the West Coast, the Armenian with eyes and ears for music like the best of us) and the ringleader, Barney Ales. I called them The Magnificent Seven.

They were an outstanding rainbow coalition with pride. All of these unsung heroes gave Motown their best, on the job and off. Their wives and children mixed and mingled with ours as we learned more about each other's cultures, hopes, and dreams.

The Motown family grew ever closer and ever stronger. Having our own sales and promotion department was expensive, but the results were worth every bit of it. We started getting crossover airplay, which meant crossover sales and crossover artists.

And the hits just kept on coming.

SIX DAY WAR

Mel, who's Arab, and Irving, who's Jewish were naturally in alliance with their respective homelands during the Six Day War between Israel and Egypt, Jordan and Syria. Of course, they had their disagreements about who was in the right. Sometimes, after a rather heated discussion, they would sit across the room from one another in silence.

On the wall behind Mel's desk, right over his head, was a painted rug of an Arab on horseback riding like the wind across the desert, with a long rifle in his hand. The painting was right out of Lawrence of Arabia. On the wall behind Irv's desk, right over his head, was a beautiful painting of the Star of David. Every now and then their eyes would meet and lock in this eye-to-eye staring combat thing, where neither one would move or turn his head first.

I would come into the office singing loud and all out of tune. "We shall overcome some day." That would break the ice. They would holler, "Get outta here!" and throw their pencils at me. It was all in fun at that point, and then I'd take them out to a soul food lunch. We would all laugh about it and talk about respecting each other's right to disagree. It was all good!

The music of Motown was growing at a pace that was unparalleled. The sound of Motown was like an ambassador of good will to people all over the world. Like the music of the Beatles, it was phenomenal!

It's hard to imagine that at the same time in South Africa and here in America, we were way outta tune! I gotta be honest with you, this segregation, racism, apartheid, Jim Crow bullshit had been building up for years, and by the time it reached the '60s, it was unbearable and totally outta control.

During the '60s we lost our friend and president, John F. Kennedy, and his brother Robert. We also lost our brother Malcolm X. All three were assassinated. In the same time span, Nelson Mandela, the anti-apartheid Black political leader, was sentenced to life in prison in South Africa.

In Birmingham, Alabama, marchers were being beaten, battered, and shot by the KKK, while the Birmingham police stayed home celebrating Mother's Day.

Birmingham became "Bombingham" after protected members of the KKK blew up the 6th Street Baptist Church, killing four innocent Black girls. They were kids, only 14 and 11 years old.

Dr. Martin Luther King, Jr., came to Detroit for a march to protest racism and segregation. He followed up with a march in Washington, DC. The world hearkened as Dr. King delivered his renowned I Have a Dream speech. Soon after, the world stood shocked and amazed at Dr. Martin King's assassination. Riots raged everywhere.

In Los Angeles, California, the riot broke out with looting and burning all around. You could hear the people screaming all the way to New York and every city in between, "Burn baby burn, burn this mother down!"

The riot that hit Newark, New Jersey, went on for six days, but the 12th Street riot in Detroit was the most incredible riot ever! Snipers turned 140 blocks into a bloody battlefield! The 12th Street riot was the worst in U. S. history.

Black homeowners in Detroit were being duped out of their property to make way for Interstate 75. After their homes had been taken away from them, they were also being told where they could and could not live. That meant you better not move your Black ass to the suburbs, if you knew what was good for you! Meanwhile, the neighborhood around 12th Street, where the rent was bearable, had grown into a huge ghetto, ready to ignite.

It all blew up when two Black soldiers celebrating their safe homecoming from Vietnam were partying at the local after hours joint, better known as the Blind Pig, on 12th Street, okay? There were 85 or more brothers and sisters partyin' down, having a good time.

At 3:30 a.m., the cops broke down the door with a sledgehammer, arrested everybody in the place and hustled them into the paddy wagons. Some onlookers were outraged at how rough the Black women were being treated. They were beaten, battered, and shoved into the wagons.

As the scene cleared and daylight broke, a dead silence fell upon the neighborhood. You could feel something was in the air. You know that eerie kinda feeling you get when you notice no one's on the street? I'm talking about an area that was seriously overpopulated.

As I looked out of my window, I not only saw the light from daybreak, but also the flames from fires being sparked in the distance. The silence had been broken as the 12th Street riot erupted. It turned Detroit, the fifth biggest city in the U.S., into a war zone! I'm talking about troops, tanks, machine guns, looting, and fires everywhere. Over 7,000 arrested and forty-two deaths. The riots in Harlem, Watts, even Newark were nothing compared to the 12th Street riot in Detroit; my own hometown - In fact in my front yard.

The Detroit News said, "It was as though the Viet Cong had infiltrated the riot-blackened streets." And my house was smack dab in the middle of the war zone. From my living room window, I could see some of my closest friends and neighbors looting and shooting. I mean, you saw brothers and sisters running for their lives, some running with new merchandise. They grabbed televisions, clothes and shoes. Some were even running with carts filled with groceries.

You're going to love this one. The owner of a music store reported losing every electric guitar, amplifier, and jazz album in the place - but the classical records were left untouched.

My friends Jerry Glassman and Kim Weston's mom were visiting me when the riot broke out. We stayed in the house and watched the riot on television. Meanwhile, my friend Jerry ate like a big dog for over a week. He must have gained ten pounds. Boy, did he love eating some soul food! Kim's mother was a great cook who loved to see you eat, and Jerry devoured soul food for days. But I'm pretty sure he was nervous as hell. When the riot was under control enough for Jerry to get the hell out of my fridge and go home to his wife, he found a way to stay for one more meal.

In Automotive News, Henry Ford II said, "I don't think there is much point in trying to sell the world on emulating our system and way of life, if we can't even put our own house in order."

With all this madness going on, Motown was marching to the beat of a different drummer. The tempo was love and respect for each other, Black or White, it didn't matter. It was not only the artists and the music; it was Motown itself and what it stood for.

Martha Crowninshield, the patrician banker at Boston Ventures, told The Hollywood Reporter's Ruth Adkins Robinson, "Motown is the Black Statue of Liberty." She thought that big, blue M was a beacon of light for everybody trying to get out of any ghetto, anywhere. She was right, too! Motown - The Sound of Young America was being heard loud and clear around the world. We were talking the talk and walking the walk; we were making a difference. It became clear to me that Motown was Berry Gordy's dream, but it was the Lord who was pulling the strings. Like my grandmother would say, "The Lord will make a way outta no way," and he did!

Not only did He give Berry the gift to hear great songs, and the eyes to see great artists, he also gave him the ability to choose the right people to do the right things at the right time. Now was the Lord pulling strings or what?

And the hits just kept on coming.

STAY - CATION

Motown was tearing down the walls of resistance with hit after hit. Barney Ales and his magnificent seven were doing their thing. The producers were producing hits, and the sales department was moving records. We had eight, sometimes ten legitimate hit records on the charts at the same time; from the number one spot down. Even Kim Weston had a hit on the charts; and she never mentioned the Dancing in the Street saga again, personally I was very proud of her – that's my girl!

I felt Kim finally began to recognize the passion I had for my work – Hey this relationship just might work out. I'd move her in with me and tighten this romance up, meet the family and all that. That's when I found out Kim's father was a preacher – not just a regular preacher but a bishop with a string of holiness churches across the South. What was it with this preacher's daughter thing and me? My first wife Betty Ann's father was a preacher – you know what? I decided from now on I'm gonna check out the family tree before I start eating the fruit, you see what I'm saying? Moving right along...

Things were going great. I was working around the clock, and it didn't bother me a bit. But evidently something was wrong because my brother Smokey kept telling me I should take a break. "You should go on vacation for a while, or something, man," he urged me.

He thought I was really pushing everybody, including myself. "Look who's calling the kettle black," I replied "you're working harder than I am. Why don't you go on vacation?"

The funny thing was, none of the producers ever went on vacation. It's not that they couldn't go; they didn't want to go. This was really about competition. What I'm saying is, even though we were a family, we were all very competitive. No producer wanted to give up the hit artist he was working on. If he was away from that artist too long, and another producer recorded a hit song on that artist, well! We would go with the hit. I went to the promotion department and had a talk with Barney Ales.

I wanted to know when he needed his next record. Barney said his hands were full for at least a month. That was great!

"Okay! Smokey," I said "I got two weeks I can spare. Where do you wanna go?" Three days later, Smokey, the Miracles and I, along with our ladies, went to Acapulco for a two-week vacation. When we arrived, we went straight to the hotel, unpacked the bags and took off to see the city.

We did everything; water skiing, scuba diving, deep sea fishing, dancing, riding, smoking, drinking, and a few other things I wouldn't care to mention, in case the women are reading this book. If Smokey hasn't told everything we did, I'm not gonna be the one to let the cat out of that bag. All I'm gonna say is, we didn't miss a thing. Trust me on that!

After being in Acapulco for just five days, mind you, Smokey and I found ourselves sitting in the hotel room, smoking some great weed and bored to death. We had seen everything there was to see and eaten everything there was to eat and - I couldn't wait to check in with the studio. I had to find out what was going on back there. As we passed the joint back and forth, looking at each other, out of nowhere and at the same time, we both said, "Let's go home."

We broke out laughing so hard we couldn't stop. It was one of those crazy laughs you get when you're high on some good pot. As soon as we came down off that Acapulco-Gold, we started packing our bags. We were ready to get the hell out of there!

The ladies were pissed off about leaving and started complaining. "Why do we have to leave now?" "This was supposed to be a vacation!" "We just got here!" But they were out ranked. While they were complaining, we were packing. Smokey and I couldn't wait to get back home so we could write songs and produce records. We even brought some of that Acapulco-Gold back with us, oh yeah! We wrapped it in some plastic and stuffed it in the ladies' make-up cream. That was cool but very stupid.

We landed in Detroit about 9 p.m. and took the limo straight to the studio. The ladies were not feeling it at all. We kissed them good-bye and told the driver to take them home. When we entered Hitsville USA, it was like stepping into heaven. We went right to work writing and producing the songs that had been on our minds from the first day we landed in Acapulco. The next thing I knew, people were coming in to work.

That meant we had been there all night - creating music.

QUALITY CONTROL AND THE INNER SANCTUM

The quality control meetings at Motown held the key to successfully achieving the Motown dream. These meetings helped form the blueprint for future African- American artists and the companies that followed.

This is the object lesson in what A&R is all about.

The quality control meetings were held once a week, unless there was an emergency meeting. This is where we picked the songs on the artists, the best mix, which artist would be released next, how they would be promoted, who would be the producer, what the album cover should look like. If you had an assignment for that meeting, that meant no excuses, no stories, and no problems were accepted. The only thing that mattered was results! As for me, I was always in the hot seat. I had to have the artists' product ready when the sales department requested it. My new secretary, Dorothy, took Martha's spot after Dancing in The Street took off and made Martha and the Vandellas one of Motown's hottest acts. Martha had one hit after another, like Jimmy Mack When Are You Coming Back, Come and Get These Memories, Heat Wave, and one of my favorites, My Baby Loves Me. Yes! I wrote that one, if that's what you're thinking.

Dorothy informed me that we had a quality control meeting coming up in a couple of days. She knew how I hated to be second-guessed in these meetings, and she wanted me to be prepared. She was right! Everyone in my department knows I am not the nicest guy in the world when the quality control meetings don't go well for me. So I decided to have my A&R meeting with my staff first. This way I could fix anything that might need fixing. I had once gone unprepared into a quality control meeting with the chairman. It was a stupid mistake I never planned to make again.

I remember it well. I was in New York at the time, for about a week, finishing up some very important business for the company. When I returned, I was called right into the quality control meeting. I wasn't worried about it because before I went to New York, I left specific instructions with everybody. I wanted all the product to be ready, overdubbed, remixed and mastered. Everything was to be on my desk by the time I got back.

Well! I came in from the airport I hit the ground running. I was already late for the meeting, so I grabbed the entire pack of product off my desk and went straight to the chairman's office, where the quality control meetings were held. When I entered the room all out of breath, everyone started congratulating me on how well I had done in New York. I was on a roll! The minutes were read and we went right into the projects that were supposed to be ready. When they got to my department, which was the most important stuff, there was something wrong with almost everything I had brought to the meeting.

For example, one of the songs was produced on the wrong artist. The song on the Marvelettes should have been on the Velvelettes, some of the mixes could have been better, the lead vocal was too low, you couldn't hear all of the words, or the background was too high. The Four Tops' new release was not ready at all and so on. If it hadn't been for my successful New York trip, my ass would have been grass.

After an early, humiliating exit from the meeting, I called all the writers and producers together and told them that we had to correct the problems like yesterday! I was determined to have every bit of product ready for the next meeting, which was in five days. We worked day and night to complete all those assignments. I was ready for the next meeting.

Only the heads of the departments were allowed to attend these meetings, and Berry Gordy himself conducted them. Believe me when I say they were always hot and heavy. The Berry Gordy who laughed and joked with us in the studio was a totally different person in the quality control meetings. That's where you met General Patton on the battlefield with guns blazing at your ass.

The chairman's motto in these meetings was, "All Gloves are Off." In other words, you could say what you felt and mean what you said to anyone and not be reprimanded for it. And baby, we had some serious knock-down, drag out discussions. You name it, we fought over it. Look! When you put a bunch of creative people in a room and you take the gloves off, the ideas will start flowing, and the heat is on.

The chairman would sit in his large black swivel chair and listen to every piece of product from beginning to end. Sometimes, without a word, he would swing his big chair around with his back to the meeting and play it again. That usually meant he liked the song, but something was not quite right. It would be totally quiet in the room; everybody would be listening to see what B.G. was listening for. The problem would either be the mix, the lead singer, or the lyrics. Sometimes the right song would be on the wrong artist.

When B.G. turned back around, the subject was open for discussion with no holds barred. After we got through the lively and heated conversations, the chairman would tell us his thoughts. Sometimes I agreed with him, and sometimes I didn't. I had one rule that always worked for me and that was, I would take the suggestions, the good ones, of course, then I'd go back in the studio and do it again.

At the next meeting, I would bring in all the copies of the songs, the original ones that were played in the first meeting and the new version with all the changes. We would listen to every one of them before making a decision. Most of the time, when the chairman made his choice, he was right! But guess what? So was I! Do you see where this is going? Well, let me help you; it was time to put your money where your mouth was.

We would bet five hundred to a thousand dollars on who was right, B.G. or me. Now you know a thousand dollars ain't nothin' to sneeze at. And I wasn't just taking anybody's word on who's right or who's wrong. No way! Not for my money. Out of the ten people in that meeting, the only people I could count on to tell the gospel truth were Smokey Robinson and Barney Ales, and that was it. Everyone else would be playing politics or sucking up to the chairman. I wasn't going for any of that bullshit. No way, José! The judges were Smokey and Barney, that's it. They wanted the best records on the streets and nothing less. Sometimes I'd win and sometimes I'd lose, but the record that went out would be a hit.

Getting airplay for Black artists was hard enough to start with, so excuses for not having the best product ready were out of the question. When Barney Ales sat in a meeting and he requested - I mean demanded - his records, all he wanted to hear was; here it is! He had his reason for wanting his product on time.

Barney's promotion staff, The Magnificent Seven, would have laid the groundwork for the record to hit the street. The radio stations were set up, the press was ready, palms were greased, and gifts were given out. And nobody, I mean nobody was gonna give anything back if the record wasn't released on time. Okay! There was a very small window of opportunity for Black artists in the first place, and a much smaller window for a Black owned record company, with Black artists.

Remember, I'm talking about the '60s here, where you better be ready with some great product and you better be on time. We didn't fool ourselves, there was a war going on out there, and The Enemies were bias, prejudice, and discrimination. We had to overcome the stranglehold of institutionalized racism on Black people in America.

Motown had a battle to win! We had to do it one artist at a time and one hit at a time. I've said it before and I'll say it again. "Motown Records was not by accident, it was by design. It took the unity of the Motown family working together, and the blessings of the good Lord, to win!"

And the hits just kept on coming.

"SPECIAL" ASSIGNMENTS

We had hits out on every artist, and my bonus had never looked better. We were on a hot run with Stevie Wonder, Smokey Robinson, The Four Tops, Martha Reeves and the Vandellas, The Contours, The Supremes, The Velvelettes, Jr. Walker and the All Stars, Kim Weston, Marvin Gaye, and Gladys Knight and the Pips. We even had the Isley Brothers on hit-street for a hot minute.

You would think I had enough to do, but not the chairman. Sometimes he would throw in a girl singer for me to produce. That's right! He would do that to me when I least expected it. Now I know it was his company and he was the boss, but I had enough to do without babysitting some no-singing chick he might be excited about for a moment. I say might because the chairman stayed too busy to get that excited.

Be that as it may, on a moment's notice he would call me into his office and introduce me to some gorgeous girl. (And I do mean gorgeous. My God! The man had great taste in women!) He would give me a special assignment to produce a demo record on her. The word "demo" was a dead giveaway. You see, it takes just as much time and effort to do a demo as it does to do a master; for that reason alone we didn't do demos. Of course, I wouldn't dare say no to the chairman, I'm not stupid!

When I received these special assignments, I would find ways to kill time with them for a week or so. If it went past a week, I knew she would be around a while. That's when I'd get to work and knock out one or two songs on the lady, just in case he asked to hear the demo. Since I was in charge of the recording budget, I did not intend to spend any more time or money than I had to.

Guess what! B.G. never expected me to do anything less. We worked it out between the two of us without saying a word. I understood what he wanted, and he understood what I was going to do.

While I'm on the subject, some of those gorgeous rejects of his, the ones that didn't last two weeks, I would find a way of keeping them around a little while longer, if you get my drift. In case you're wondering, none of this product ever got to a quality control meeting, no way! That was not business. That was strictly personal, okay?

I decided not to take any more vacations for a while and that decision did not sit too well with Kim Weston. I tried being a more romantic and understanding kinda guy; I changed my whole routine. I would come home from the studio and spend quality time relaxing with her.

We would have a glass of champagne, small talk, watch TV, or whatever. I gotta tell you this was not working for me. If we didn't throw in some kinda hot lovemaking, I would be bored to death.

During one of my boring yet relaxing TV evenings - I remember it was way past late - I heard brakes pulling a car to a stop right outside my door. My doorbell started ringing like crazy and someone started banging on my door. You can't imagine how excited I was to see Barney Ales, half drunk and pissed off. It seems somebody was bootlegging our records up in Harlem. It took me thirty minutes and a bottle of my best brandy to calm him down.

Now, Barney could hold his liquor, no matter how much he drank. He was still only half way loaded. "Okay, Barney, calm down!" I said, "So someone is bootlegging our records in New York, so what's the big deal?"

In Harlem! He said, "And I'll tell you what the big deal is. Nobody can bootleg my records and get away with it."

I had a feeling this was about to go the wrong way. All of a sudden Barney's voice sounded as if he had sobered up. He said, "You're going to New York to find out who's bootlegging our records, and if it's who we think it is, the shit's gonna hit the fan!"

I was taken by surprise. "You want me to go to New York?"

Without hesitation, Barney said, "Yeah, you! What do you think I 'm doing here at this hour, visiting?"

I calmly let him have it. "Hey, Barney baby, I'm Mickey Stevenson, the A&R man, remember? Not Shaft, the private eye."

Barney laughed. "Hey, slick Mick! I knew who you were before you became the A&R man, so cut the crap. We want you to go back to Harlem to some of those friends of yours, and find out what's going on."

"We" was the key word. It meant the chairman and Barney had worked this thing all out. They probably knew who was doing the bootlegging but they just needed more proof, and that's where I came in. They both knew I was hooked up with some of the boys in Harlem from the days of the Apollo Motown tour. I would see the boys every time I went to the Big Apple. Those brothers up in Harlem knew how to party.

I took the next flight to New York, first class. I was determined to make this trip as comfortable as possible. The Warwick Hotel was my favorite stop in New York, but this time I needed a little more flash, and a lot more room. I called my friend at the Hilton, who was one of the managers. He was a good songwriter, too. I told him what I needed and he knew just what to do. As soon as I checked into the lavish suite he gave me, I called some of my boys in Harlem. Nothing moved on the streets in Harlem that they were not aware of, or had a piece of. We had dinner in my room, while I explained my problem. I told the boys I had a week to find out who was bootlegging my records.

It only took the boys about eight hours to come up with the answer. They told me who was doing it and how they were doing it. So I spent the next couple of days partying with the boys at the hotel. They would not let me off that easy. Bumpy, my main man, insisted that I come down to Harlem and stay at his place for a few days. He wanted the rest of the 'hood to meet his friend from Motown Records. Hey! I was a big man in Harlem! We partied down all day and every night for the rest of the week. Between you and me, I had a hell of a time.

On my flight home, I figured it out - if I found out who was bootlegging our records that fast, it only confirmed my suspicion that B.G. and Barney knew who it was, too. Barney had his connection in New York, and his friends didn't live in Harlem, if you know what I mean. Needless to say, the bootlegging stopped.

I was sent back to New York, this time to produce an album on an artist for the godfather of the record business, Morris Levy. He owned Roulette Records, and he was one of Barney's friends who didn't live in Harlem. I was doing a favor for Barney and I suspected it was in connection with the bootleg caper. You know - a favor for a favor.

Now the godfather had a reputation of getting things done one way or another. The day I walked into his office at Roulette Records, it was like a scene out of the movies. There he was, "the godfather" sitting in a huge black leather chair behind an outsized desk with one of those fat, expensive-looking cigars in his mouth. There were five or six guys, all in dark suits and ties, standing around. It was a little intimidating. I didn't know what to expect. Everybody in the place was huge, including Nate McAllen, the Black promotion man who worked for the godfather. Nate was a mountain of a man, over six feet, and he must have weighed more than three hundred pounds. He stood there looking like Sonny Liston with a hat on. Did I say I was intimidated? That was not quite the right choice of words. Let's try scared! Yeah, scared fits the moment quite nicely. Morris Levy spoke in that deep whiskey-like voice of his. "How you doing? How was your trip? Is your room OK?"

Before I could say a word, he must have asked me ten questions. Somehow, he had a way of making you feel relaxed. I think it was his laugh, yeah! That was it. He had a big laugh that went along with his big smile, his deep voice, and that mega-cigar. I liked him, and he must have liked me, too. We talked about his artist. He even invited me out to his farm where he had some Black Angus cows. I had no idea what a Black Angus cow was.

I thought this was the perfect time to ask him a very important question. "Suppose you don't like what I produce on your artist. How do I leave the farm?" Morris hit the desk with his fist, looked at me, and broke out laughing. He laughed so hard he almost choked on his cigar. "This is a funny guy!" he said. "How do you like this guy? He's been watching too many gangster movies."

All of his boys started laughing. I couldn't control myself and I started laughing, too. Morris, still laughing, looked at me and said, "I really like this guy!"

"I like you too, Morris," I said, "but I'm still not going out to your ranch." We all must have laughed another two minutes. I must admit Uncle Morris (as they called him) took very good care of me while I was in New York recording his artist. He sure knew how to treat a guy. When I got back to the office in Detroit, Barney told me Uncle Morris liked the song I'd produced on his artist, and I was selected to do an album of songs from Morris' publishing catalog. I was to produce an album on Marvin Gaye and the girls of Motown, and I could pick my own songs. I was surprised to see he had some great standards in his catalog, some of the songs I had sung when I was on the road with the Hamptones and the Four Freshmen. This may have been Motown's way of returning a favor, but the pleasure was all mine.

I had a chance to put the Motown sound to some standards. The Funk Brothers loved it, too. We had a ball recording that album. When Uncle

Morris heard the album, he called me personally to tell me that he loved it. I really enjoyed that compliment.

I didn't find out what a Black Angus cow was until years later.

'

COMPANY SONG

I had the A&R department humming like a bird and running like a well-oiled machine. It couldn't get any better than this. I even cut out the poker games that went on almost every night between sessions, and you know that hurt me since I was always the biggest winner. I would easily win two to four thousand a week. I had I.O.Us all over the place. You could pay me now or when you got your royalty check. I didn't mind waiting; it was all good.

The problem with the poker games started when some of the producers and artists started asking for advances to play poker. That meant the poker games were becoming more important than the sessions, and that's one thing I couldn't afford. I called a meeting of all the players and told them that the card games were over. I also told them why they were over. Even though it broke my heart and my pockets weren't too happy about it either, I took all the I.O.Us and tore them up! It was back to business.

The Motown writers and producers enjoyed challenging each other. As I said earlier, we were all very competitive. We would challenge one another to come up with the best song, or the best background, right down to the best hook, or bridge to a song, and we'd bet on it. We had marvelous creative battles going on, day and night. The greatest thing about this competitive spirit was that, as we competed with one another, striving to have the best songs, we all got better. The product got better, we sold more records, and I made more money. And you know I loved that! What a wonderful time that was. Whenever important visitors were invited to one of our company meetings, they could feel the positive energy the moment they walked through the door at Motown. They could feel it even more so when they heard us sing the company song. Oh yeah! We had our own company song, and when we sang it, all of our voices would become one, and we had some great voices. Each verse grew stronger and stronger as if it were spiritually inspired. It was another one of the main threads that held us together. It gave you the secure feeling that you were part of the Motown family. We would open every company meeting with our song.

When B.G. came up with the idea of a company song and asked Smokey to write it, personally I thought it was a little over the top, and to be honest with you even a little corny.

It reminded me of some of those movies where the soldiers are marching off to war and they don't know if they're gonna survive or not. As they march into battle they're passionately singing the company song. You know what I mean. That kind of crap!

Boy was I wrong!

And, man, was he right!

The song worked like a charm, just like in the movies! Even I learned to love that song. The visitors would be in awe when they heard us singing it. The last verse would get 'em every time. In those earliest days, we were showing people in the industry, artists, and others, that unity among Black people was a reality.

And the hits just keep on coming.

"Oh we are a very swinging company
Working hard from day to day
Nowhere would you find more unity
Than at Hitsville, I said Hitsville
Than at Hitsville, U S A"

BLACK ARTISTS ON TV

The consensus among the white agencies was that Black talent was cheap talent. This bigoted attitude allowed for only a few exceptions, like Nat King Cole, who was a smooth, stylized singer. His articulation of song lyrics was impeccable. He even had his own half hour TV show for a minute. Harry Belafonte, on the other hand, was tall and handsome, with a figure like a Greek statue. With his open shirt and sexy island songs, Harry had women of all colors all over the world adoring him. They considered him someone other than a Black man. Go figure that! Artists like Count Basie, Duke Ellington, Ray Charles and Billie Holiday had an uphill battle getting some of what they were worth, compared to their white counterparts. This was consistent with the times we lived in.

With America still going through its maze of racist turmoil, it also had the Hispanics to contend with. Their numbers were growing faster and faster. Religious and spiritual Black people were soul searching as to which leader they would follow. Some flocked to Malcolm X, while others were led by Dr. Martin Luther King's protégé, the charismatic Rev. Jesse Jackson. The boycotts were going on, and change had begun.

As civil rights groups gained more and more white support, whites were being jailed right along with the Blacks. The Blacks were saying, "I am somebody." James Brown said, "Say it loud, I'm Black and I'm proud." America's Walls of Jericho, built on prejudices and hatred, were beginning to tumble down. This was happening with the voices of young America speaking out. Some of the voices were listening to the sounds of Motown. I feel the music of Motown helped bring some healing to our nation. It brought all kinds of people together; Native Americans, Asians, Hispanics, and Caucasians crossing all cultures through the love of music. It was obvious, particularly among the young people.

Through all that revolutionary movement, the Motown family grew bigger and stronger. We had artists coming out with both barrels firing, artists like Junior Walker's Shotgun (Shoot 'em fore he run now), Gladys Knight and the Pips' I Heard It Through the Grapevine, Smokey Robinson, The Temptations, The Four Tops. The Supremes were leading the pack with another number one record. By the way, these same Motown fans turned out to be the mothers, fathers, even grandparents of today. If you don't believe me, ask your parents. They're still around, right? And they still love the sound of Motown.

The movies and the TV networks stood their ground against Blacks for a long time. Sometimes they graciously allowed some Black artists to appear on their shows to perform one song. The network would make this big announcement that Al Green or Aretha Franklin or maybe Otis Redding or The Temptations would be on at eight o'clock on a given night. Man! Black people all over America would run out to the stores and buy some beer, some potato chips with the hot dip, some strawberry soda, and a bottle of Ripple red wine, baby! They would be ready!

They'd invite some friends over, grab a good seat in front of the twelve-inch TV, and wait for their favorite artist to come on. They found themselves waiting and waiting and waiting. The beer would be all gone, the chips and dip finished, and the TV show almost over. Don't you dare get up and go to the bathroom - 'cause if you did, not only would you miss your favorite artists, but the credits would be rolled out while the artist was singing, and the show would be over. I mean, that's all folks.

Now let me tell you how Motown helped change the disrespectful treatment of Black artists on TV. It all started with The Supremes, who were the number one girl group in the world. To be number one in the world, you had to have more than Black consumers buying your records, right? Right! Everybody wanted The Supremes on their TV shows, even Ed Sullivan, who had the number one show in America. The chairman's office talked to the Ed Sullivan office and it went like this; The Supremes were not to be put on last, and they would have a chance to talk to Ed Sullivan on camera, and they would sing two songs. They all agreed.

But when Gil Askey, the Supremes' conductor, arrived at the Ed Sullivan show for rehearsal, he was told he could not rehearse or conduct the orchestra. Sullivan's staff told Gil that the Ed Sullivan Orchestra could only be conducted by their own people. The feeling was, no one else would lord it over this all white orchestra, not on your life. Just leave the music and go away.

Here we go again with some more of the good old white supremacy nonsense. Gil called the chairman, B.G. and gave him the bad news. The chairman got on the phone to Ed Sullivan's people and said,

"No Gil Askey, no Supremes." B.G. stood up for the Motown artists, producers and writers.

Gil was called back in to conduct for The Supremes. When he finished rehearsing the orchestra on the arrangements that he wrote, all the musicians applauded him. They gave Gil the respect he deserved, and why not? The man is a fantastic arranger and conductor.

I ought ta' know; I picked him.

RUMORS & MYTHS

While we're on the subject of respect, let's clear up some of the myths and rumors about Motown's talented writers and producers. I'm talking about the ones who wrote the hits the world loves.

As a writer myself, I can tell you that many of the tales being told are outright lies. For example, there's a story out that Motown didn't pay royalties to the songwriters. It was even said that Motown stole the writers' songs. What utter nonsense, garbage. As the A&R man, I not only signed the artists and producers to Motown, I also signed writers to Jobete, the publishing company. I signed the writers who wrote all the songs that the producers produced and the artists sang.

Stevie Wonder, Marvin Gaye, The Four Tops, The Temptations, The Supremes, Martha Reeves, The Vandellas, Gladys Knight and the Pips - I can go through the whole roster of hit artists at Motown if you like. The point is, you need hit songs to have hit artists, and you need good writers to write hit songs. Are you staying with me here? Good!

If you wrote a song for a Motown artist, your song was published by Jobete, which became one of the most powerful music publishers in the business. All the writers I signed to Jobete had the gift and the ability to excel. Some of them even had the potential to be great writers. Sometimes I would be lucky enough to find talented people who had the potential to do all three; sing, produce, and write. Triple threats! Working with these talented people is where the A&R man becomes the coach, mentor, father, teacher and friend. If you're wondering how I decided who to sign and who not to sign, I'll tell you.

I would have each writer sing his best original song, the song that made him believe he was a songwriter. If I liked the song, I would have him sing another song. This time he would have to name which Motown artists he thought the song would suit.

If I reached this point in the audition, not only was I listening to the songs, I'd be listening and looking for the writer's commitment, focus, vision and determination. The writers with these character traits and work ethic would stick out like a sore thumb. I would not hesitate to sign them. I would get totally involved in the development of a triple threat. Most of the writers and producers were given a weekly advance. This was our way of giving them support and encouragement.

All of them had the opportunity to work with other writers and producers as they developed their skills. Even the artists would get into the act when a song was written for them. This was a family affair and everybody played a part. This dispels fabrications, about songs being stolen or taken from writers at Motown. The writers and producers all worked together. They learned from one another, sharing creative ideas, words, background, tempos and hooks. All the writers had a chance to have their songs produced and recorded on the Motown artist. If a writer or producer had a hit on the artist, they automatically had first option on the follow-up record on that artist. I love being right about an artist, a producer or a writer; about a creative person, period. I'm the kind of guy who gets absolutely committed and driven.

I loved watching them develop. I'm telling you, I really loved it! And to discover a triple threat, too. Yes! That was the ultimate discovery. I get all worked up just thinking about it. Now let me make this clear. Jobete Publishing Company has been paying royalties to its writers for more than 50 years and is still paying. Jobete Publishing, in its own way, was a vision of pride and unity. No songs were ever taken or stolen, not on my watch.

Now get to this! Do you remember Martha Crowninshield, the banker at Boston Ventures? Anyway, Martha was good at assessing value. She orchestrated the purchase of Motown from B.G. She bought the Motown catalogue for $61 million and sold it five years later for $325 million. Now that's a good assessment. Because of the sale of the Motown catalogue to Universal, and Jobete Publishing Company to EMI, the writers are receiving more royalties now than ever before. And Motown Records is celebrating over 55 years of music. And the hits just keep on coming.

There are a few ways writers and artists get paid for making records. Advances, of course, are one way. Mechanical royalties are another. The mechanical royalties are paid to both writers and artists. This money comes from actual record sales.

There are also the performance royalties; that's when your record gets played on the radio, on TV or in a movie, for example. With radio airplay, the payment is made to the writers of the songs. With visual outlets like movies and TV, payments could be made to artists, writers, and the record company. For the longest time, there was only one worthwhile agency doing all the collecting for performance royalties. That was the American Society of Composers, Authors and Publishers (ASCAP).

ASCAP's main interest was in the writers of show tunes, pop songs, classical music and so forth. The agency didn't show the same enthusiasm for signing Black R & B music writers as they did for writers of country music, gospel and even rock and roll music, these writers had no agency to collect royalties for their songs. Then along came Broadcast Music, Incorporated (BMI), which gladly took on the new generation of writers and their bold music. The new generation of listeners made this music hot, too! Really hot! Suddenly the sound on the radio changed. Many of the big records on the charts were Motown songs, along with other hit artists of the new generation.

The writers of this hot R&B music signed with BMI, and their songs were dominating the airwaves. According to Robin Cartwright of Straight Dope Science Advisory Board (paraphrasing his quotes) ASCAP accused BMI of using payola to ensure airplay for BMI songs and writers. There are arguments to be made on both sides of the question. Maybe the scandal wasn't as much about race as it was about power and money. Some contend that payola helped smaller labels break the majors' stranglehold on the market, and the scandal offered a way to fight back.

Getting the Records On, Keeping the Records On.

As I said before, there were only a few people in the record companies, artists included, who had a clue about how the product even got on the air. Some didn't care how it got on. The rest were completely oblivious. It was a matter of math.

At that time, a major record company might release upwards of fifteen singles a week. Independent labels like Motown didn't release anything like that. And when you add an R & B artist to the roster, imagine how hard it was for the labels to get the stations just to pay attention to their product. It was really a trip. Maybe ten percent of all the singles released in any given week would end up making a profit - by selling records from the radio exposure.

Now get to this! A radio station's playlist consisted of 36 to 40 records a week. This playlist would be rotated every hour for a week or more. According to the sales, or to the response from listeners calling the station and requesting more airplay ("Play that song again!"), some records would be taken off the playlist, and new records added on. The record labels had to figure out a way to get their records on that station's playlist. The labels hired promoters who paid deejays to put the record on their stations and keep it in rotation.

So bribery, payola, call it whatever you like, it took more than just a hit record to make airplay happen.

And you can take that to the bank.

THE BEGINNING OF THE END

The first crack in the Motown armor came at a time when I least expected it, and in a way I never suspected. Let's see if I can lay this out for you without getting too emotional.

Let's start with the production team of Holland-Dozier-Holland (H.D.H.). They were the hottest producers at Motown and, I would venture to say, in the world. With The Supremes selling more records than any girl group in the world, H.D.H. was on a roll. They were number one, Smokey Robinson was number two, and yours truly was number three. Then came; Marvin Gaye, Norman Whitfield, Ivy Jo Hunter, Barrett Strong, Harvey Fuqua, and Johnny Bristol.

I had other producers, but these were the main ones. The position between the third, fourth and fifth would constantly change at Motown, according to the hits that came out. But the number one and number two spots stayed pretty much the same, Holland-Dozier-Holland and Smokey Robinson.

The best part of this whole deal for me was that, as A&R director, I got an override. That meant I received a royalty from every record that went out; it didn't matter who produced it. The bigger the hit, the more money I made. I did my best to encourage everyone to do their best. I would even give up my spot on an artist to other producers, if I felt it would inspire them to do greater things. As the A&R man, I was in a no-lose position.

Eddie Holland, the older brother on the fantastic H.D.H. production team, was also its leader and spokesperson. He was very quiet and soft spoken; an introvert with a huge ego, and I do mean huge.

Like the rest of us, he had a very competitive nature, and it was backed up with a driving force that pushed the other two members of his team. Eddie wrote most of the lyrics and cracked the whip for H.D.H. Whenever I needed my songs from H.D.H. for the quality control meetings or the promotion department, I'd talk to Eddie, and he'd get his brother Brian and Lamont on the ball; he had control.

Lamont Dozier was a brilliant writer and a hopeless romantic. The way he would create the rhythms for the songs was outstanding. He wrote the greatest song hooks ever, the hooks you find yourself singing along with every time you hear them Baby love, my baby love, Missin' you, miss kissin' you, Stop in the name of love, before you break my heart, Sugar Pie Honey Bunch, you know that I love you, you know the rest. On one hand, Lamont's romantic heart kept him in trouble with his personal life. On the other hand, it did wonders for his creative life. If you need evidence, just look at the music he created. Lamont's romantic entanglements were the motivation that helped him write such great songs. What I'm saying is the songs came straight from his heart.

Brian Holland, Eddie's younger brother, was, like Eddie, an introvert. He also was an all-around creative genius. He could write, produce, play a mean piano, and sing. He always seemed to be in a world of his own. The difference between the two brothers was that Brian had a sympathetic and giving nature, a real soft spot. The ladies considered him a teddy bear. A sad story would get to him every time. Now Benny Benjamin, our drummer with the drug problem, man! Did he love him some Brian Holland! Every time Benny saw Brian he would lay one of his sad "I need" stories on Brian, and guess what? Brian, with his gentle soul and soft heart, would go for it every time. It's not that Brian believed Benny, he just felt so sorry for him. You see what I mean?

Neither Brian nor Lamont minded Eddie doing all the talking for H.D.H. That way, they could stay out of the mix and clear of any pressure. Eddie, the leader and thinker, was beginning to feel his oats. He wanted more than just a royalty as a producer and writer. Eddie wanted some of Motown and was out to get it. He started applying pressure on the chairman for a bigger piece of the pie.

Now let's look at this thing from Eddie Holland's point of view. Holland-Dozier-Holland was one of the hottest production teams in the world, barring none other than maybe The Beatles. H.D.H had at least half a dozen songs on the charts and all over the radio, written and produced by H.D.H. Even the Beatles sang songs written by Holland, Dozier, and Holland.

In 1964, the number one hits they wrote and produced on The Supremes alone were unprecedented; Baby Love, Come See About Me, and Where Did Our Love Go, were all by The Supremes, all written and produced by the team of H.D.H. Not to mention all their other hits on artists such as Marvin Gaye, The Four Tops, Martha and the Vandellas. Even Kim Weston became a hot artist because of H.D.H. When you looked at the financial growth of the Motown record empire, not to mention Jobete, the publishing company, Brother Eddie had a point.

Eddie felt H.D.H. was one of the leading contributors to the Motown dynasty, and he wanted a bigger payoff. And that's the name of that tune.

Now, H.D.H. contracts were coming up for renewal, and Eddie wasn't about to lighten up on his demands for more of the Motown pie. Not on your life! Being an introvert didn't make him a dummy.

Eddie's threats of leaving the company and taking Holland, Dozier, and Holland with him didn't sit too well with the chairman. So the battle was on! Eddie was determined to get some publishing and a bigger royalty, and the chairman had to find a way to satisfy Eddie, keep Holland-Dozier-Holland, and not give up any of his Motown dynasty.

There was even a bigger problem in this saga - egos! Eddie Holland had a huge ego, as one of the hottest producers and writers in the world, and B.G., his ego goes without saying after building the fastest growing recording and publishing company ever. Come to think about it, even I had a slight ego, as the A&R director and mentor for the hottest young artists, writers, and producers in the world.

When ego gets involved, logic and understanding can get trampled. A wrong decision made under those circumstances could start a fire that could burn down the house. A decision had to be made, and soon!

The chairman called me to his office for a meeting. I knew something was wrong because at the very beginning of the meeting he started stumbling for words to say to me. I couldn't believe it. This was not like him, no way! What I mean is, when the chairman had something to say to you, he would lay it on you straight up, take it or leave it. For the first time in our relationship, I saw Berry Gordy stumble around for words to say to me.

He found a way to tell me that he was promoting me to the office of the president. I was getting a new office and another secretary, and I was receiving a raise in pay. He told me that he wanted me to work on some special project for him. I asked him what kind of project he had in mind. "We might try our hand in some Broadway musical shows; let's see what's out there," he said. "I want you to start looking around right away."

Wow! I didn't know what to say. I liked it. The only thing was, I didn't want to leave my department right then, not to go looking for some Broadway shows. So I said, "Okay, B.G., but I'm gonna need some time to set my department in order. The last time I went away for a week, everything went crazy."

The famous half smile made an appearance. He said, "I have someone to handle the A&R department."

I was astounded. "What? Who? What are you saying to me? Is this a joke or something?"

That's when he told me he had already given Eddie Holland my position as the head of A&R. I was dumbfounded. To this day I remember the uncomfortable feeling I had. First came the shock, which turned into hurt, and then the disappointment set in. I didn't know what to say. I stood there in disbelief. It also hit me that the "special projects" bit was merely a ploy; this was his way of making it easier on me.

All I could think about was, that's my position, I'm the A&R man, I built this department into what it is, and now it's all being taken away from me and turned over to Eddie Holland. Man! I couldn't believe it! I was the sacrificial lamb. It wasn't supposed to look that way, with this "special project" bullshit, but that's exactly what it was. Personally, I thought it was a terrible decision.

B.G. went on to say that Eddie would be taking over right away, and that he may need my help getting it all together. My help! Wow! That was really asking an awful lot of me. You see what I'm saying? That was pushing it to the brink!

At that point I could tell B.G. had made up his mind, and anything I'd say from there would only make the situation more painful for both of us. It was clear that I was one of B.G.'s greatest accomplishments. Not only did I become the A&R man that he knew I could be, but I had gone beyond his expectations to become a leader and mentor, one of the unsung heroes of Motown. Like I said in the beginning, Motown was and still is a very important part of my life.

Everything that you've read so far has been seen through my eyes and my heart as Motown's first A&R man. What happened from that point on is going to be rather difficult for me to write about. Just thinking about it still hurts, but here goes!

Eddie Holland was a loner like I said, not the people person the A&R job required. Let me rephrase that; the A&R job demanded!

Being an A&R executive was more than teaching an artist a song or producing a record; that was easy compared to what this position required. The A&R department at Motown demanded much more than what Eddie was willing to give.

Now if I knew this, it stands to reason that B.G. knew this as well. What in the world was he thinking about, putting Eddie in that position?

At first I thought maybe it was because the A&R department was running so well, nobody could screw it up; not even Eddie. Then I thought about the growth of the company. The new artists, the up and coming young talented singers, writers, and producers - they were what Motown would need. They were the ones who would keep the energy flowing - and the company growing.

Eddie was not going out of his way to scout for anybody and that included new young talent. If they didn't come walking through the door, they were just flat out of luck, and so was Motown. Eddie Holland is a writer/producer first and foremost, not a mentor for young talented artists. That takes a special kind of person; even I knew that. The A&R man's responsibilities are not only to find new talent, but to groom and work with them as well.

A&R is the lifeline of all record companies, not just Motown. All these things were running through my head as I watched the chairman talk. I could see his mouth moving, but my thoughts were somewhere else. I was thinking, man, Holland-Dozier-Holland's contracts were running out, and I'm sure they were getting offers from other companies. Yeah! That's it. Hell, I was getting offers from companies every other week and I did not intend to leave Motown. I concluded that Eddie must have given him an ultimatum. B.G. had to make Eddie Holland the A&R director or Holland-Dozier-Holland was gonna walk. That had to be it. Yeah! It was strictly business. That's what I kept telling myself so that I could keep working at Motown. I must admit Holland-Dozier-Holland were the hottest producers in the country at the time. I should know; I helped put them there. You could say that I helped create the monster that turned on me.

As for Berry's decision to make Eddie the A&R man, what the hell, I probably would have done the same thing if I'd been in his shoes... well, maybe not. I wouldn't have gotten rid of me (Now you see what an ego can do.)

I left the chairman's office mad as hell, disappointed and disillusioned. I called all the writers, producers and the musicians together to make my farewell speech as A&R director. I had to keep my composure as I spoke. It wasn't easy turning everything over to Eddie, and I could see the strange looks on everyone's faces, from shock to confusion. By the time I finished speaking, everyone seemed to be okay with it.

Everyone, but yours truly.

A CHANGE IS GON' COME

Not being the A&R man anymore wasn't too bad. What the hell, I didn't have to listen to everybody's problems anymore or be bothered with keeping the musicians out of every other studio in town. Even the drummer Benny Benjamin was out of my hair.

Working out of the president's office was supposed to be exciting, but if you wanna know the truth, sitting in my office answering phone calls about the A&R department was really getting to me. Listening to everyone complain didn't help my situation at all. If it wasn't the artists it was the musicians bellyaching about money. Even the producers were calling me. This was driving me crazy!

The fact is; there was really nothing I could do about any of it. All I could say to them was, "Everything will be all right. Just give it some time." All the while, I knew it was not gonna work. You see, Eddie didn't give a damn about the job. All he wanted was the money and a piece of the pie. This was a very uncomfortable time in my life. It seemed as though everything that could go wrong was going wrong and it was all happening at the same time.

My position at Motown was on shaky ground; my ex-wife was busting my balls with her lawyers, going after all the money she could squeeze out of me. On top of all that, Kim Weston's biological clock was ticking, and she was constantly giving me marriage dialogue which I was really not ready for. My writing and producing was producing absolutely nothing. Man, I couldn't stay focused. I didn't know how I was holding it all together.

The real question was, why didn't I just walk out of there? Who was I kidding? I know why I didn't walk out, and I couldn't walk out. Besides, I felt Motown would be losing a part of its musical formula for success.

I know it was quite presumptuous of me to think that, but along with the hurt, that's the way I felt. Like I said in the beginning, Motown was a huge part of my life.

If you've ever been in a position where you felt your value had been depreciated, then you know the feeling. If you've never been there, consider yourself one of the lucky ones. All this mental babbling I was putting myself through was nothing but denial.

I was simply denying the fact that I was no longer needed. I had done my job too well. The Motown A&R department could run without Mickey Stevenson. With all that said, I still wanted to be around to pick up the pieces when Eddie dropped the ball. I'd step up to the plate and save the day, just like in the movies. Only this was not the movies, this was real life, and this was not gonna happen. As Stevie Wonder once sang, "Everything must change, nothing stays the same."

All I could do was hope the change would be for the betterment of Motown. As hurt and as bitter as I was, I really loved that place and everyone in it, including Eddie Holland. Motown was my family. I finally got up enough nerve to go to Berry and tell him how I was feeling. I was seriously thinking about resigning from the company and I felt I owed him an explanation. I wanted to talk face to face. I was hoping he'd find a reason to have me stay around, especially for my sake. The chairman was very concerned as he listened to me. He seemed to understand my frustration and he even asked me not to leave. "What would it take for you to stay? The company needs you, and we should be able to work something out."

Well! After hearing him talk like that, I felt pretty good and, with a smile on my face and joy in my heart, I told the chairman that I would think about it. He said, "No problem! Take the rest of the week off, and we'll talk about it later."

I walked away feeling pretty good. I remember thinking what would it take for me to stay. I knew I wasn't going to get the A&R department back, not right away, even though Eddie Holland was not gonna last and that was a fact, too. I also knew that I couldn't just sit around listening to the artists and writers complain all day, either. It was quite a dilemma.

Instead of going home that night, I went out and had a couple of drinks, maybe more. I was still not ready to go home and listen to Kim, so I went back to the studio and jumped on the piano. I'll work this thing out through a song, I thought. It was déjà vu, the same kinda soul searching I had gone through when I was living in that shabby apartment over Denny's Show Bar. How ironic! After all these years, here I was, at the piano, trying to write my way out of a problem. I had come full circle.

After sitting at the piano for at least an hour or more, trying to write something, the chairman came in. He stood watching me.

"What's that you're working on? It sounds pretty good!" He walked over, sat down next to me and started playing some new chord to the song I was working on. He came up with some good stuff; we had a creative thing going on for a moment. There we were, working together as if nothing had ever happened. He worked with me on the song for a few more minutes, and then he said he had to leave.

About ten minutes later he came back to the studio in a panic. "Did you see that envelope I had when I came in here?"

"Envelope?" I said, looking around. "What envelope?" The look on his face told me it must have been important. We both started looking for it. I found it on the floor right next to the piano. When I handed him the envelope, he opened it immediately.

"Do you know what's in here?" Before I could say no, he pulled out a bunch of cashier's checks, worth thousands of dollars. He counted them, breathed a sigh of relief and left the studio.

I stayed a little while longer trying to finish the song that he and I had worked on, but it wasn't happening. My creative juices were gone! All I could think about was that envelope with all those thousands of dollars in cashier's checks. It struck me then, sitting at the piano where I'd begun my creative journey that I was in the wrong end of this business.

I couldn't sleep at all that night just thinking about it. Even Kim and all her complaining didn't faze me a bit that night; it was all about that money, honey. I had a decision to make and I knew it would never be the same for me after that.

You see, it all came together for me at once. All the love in the world wouldn't change the fact that if you wanna be in charge of your own destiny, you have to take charge. If you wanna make that kinda money, brother, you have to have your own business. The circumstances had brought on a revelation; a new dimension had been added to my life. The idea may have been there all the time, but I never thought about nurturing it until that moment. I had no reason, no desire; I had never given it a thought. I had felt safe and secure with Motown, and there'd been no reason to think about doing anything else.

Unforeseeable circumstances had painfully brought me to the realization that there is no such thing as safe and secure; it's a myth. The only things you can count on that won't change are death and the word of God

Almighty. It was all I thought about for the rest of the night. I knew that if I wanted to feel any kind of security at all, I better start doing my own thing.

It was becoming clearer to me that all the things I had learned from my early years with the Hamptones, Bobby Day, running the gospel label, and even the road tours, right up to the Motown phenomenon, were for a purpose. All of it had been a prelude, a kind of overture to fulfilling my own destiny. In other words, it was my time to use my own wings and take flight. It's a mystery to me how God prepares you for something without you ever knowing it.

Now I had learned that ambitious movements without knowledge can be very dangerous. But it was time, and without taking the step, that leap of faith, you'll never know what God has in store for you. The chairman and I had our meeting the following day. He asked me what it would take to make me stay with the Motown family. I felt very comfortable as I explained to him that I had thought about it, and the only thing that would work for me would be to have some stock in Motown records and a piece of the publishing company.

I explained to him that I needed this for my future and the future of my kids. This way I would not only be working for the company but I'd also be working for myself.

For a moment, B.G. was taken aback. But he recovered, and calmly said to me, "I can't do that. I know you helped to make Motown and Jobete, but so did a lot of other people around here, and if I gave you some stock, I'd have to give them some, too.

"B.G., I'm not talking about the other people; I'm talking about you and me."

He said it again. "I can't do that, but I'll tell you what I will do. I'll up your salary. That's the best I can do, how's that?"

I knew by the way he looked and by the way he said it, he was making this benevolent offer because giving me some stock in Motown or Jobete was out of the question. We both knew from that moment on it was all over.

If I was going to build a future for myself, I had to do it just like he did, get out there and do my own thing. Sure I was one of Motown's unsung heroes, but the fact remains I didn't own any of the company and I wasn't about to get any of it, either. The best thing I could do was stop wasting time, get out there and start building my own. I told him I appreciated the offer to raise my salary, but that was not the answer I was looking for. I gave the chairman my two-week notice, and he accepted it. We shook hands and he gave me a big Motown hug.

While holding me, he said, "You'll do great. Just remember all you've learned. If you need anything, anything at all - don't hesitate to call me."

"I just might have to do that, chief, sooner than you think."

As I walked out of his office, the chairman said, "I want you to do me a favor."

"Sure, Chief, you name it."

With a rather serious look on his face, he said, "I only ask one thing of you. Don't make any press releases of a negative nature about Motown."

I couldn't believe he'd said that to me! I told him without hesitation, "You didn't have to ask me that, B. G. The happiest part of my life was spent right here. I happen to love this company and you too, for giving me the opportunity to be part of it. There is nothing I could tell anybody but the truth, and that is the truth." He knew I meant what I said. He smiled as we gave each other another good-bye hug.

I stuck to my word on that press release thing. Not only did I not say anything negative about Motown, but I would not allow anyone else to say anything negative about the company, the family or the chairman, not in my presence. No way!

The chairman stuck to his word, too. Every time I called him for some help, it was a done deal. By the way, I asked the chairman for Kim Weston's contract. Kim and Marvin Gaye had a hit record, *It Takes Two*, that was flying up the charts at the time. Without hesitation, he gave it to me. Right up to this day, he has never gone back on his word to me. But I'm getting ahead of myself again. Where was I? Oh, yeah! I was leaving the company.

Now, whenever I fired someone or put someone out of Motown, I would have a security guard walk him or her out of the building. They couldn't take anything with them except for the pink slip. When I left, the chairman let me take whatever I wanted or needed. Nobody followed me around or even asked me any questions. In fact, when I was ready to leave the building, I turned in my own keys.

As I was walking out the door of Hitsville USA, it felt like I was going on a vacation. You know, like when you love your family and everything, but you need a break from them. That's how I felt. I was also very proud that I was a part of the team that had developed the sound that was heard around the world. We made a difference in people's lives and because of the Motown success story - Black artists on other labels were being noticed for their talent, not for the color of their skin.

The rhythm and blues train was on the move and nothing on earth could stop it. Black artists in all fields of entertainment were becoming a force to be reckoned with, thank God for that!

The Motown alumni stayed in touch over the years. There were a few who went crazy, but you got a couple crazies in every family.

Whenever we encountered one another, it was as if we'd never parted.

STEVENSON VS. STEVENSON

Moving right along! By this time, my first wife was hitting me up for more alimony and child support. Early on, I remember standing in front of the judge as he looked over my tax records. He looked down at me. "You make more money than I do," he said. My lawyer and I knew we were in trouble.

Every year, my ex would put on the saddest clothes she could find. She would apply make-up that gave her a homely, Gloria Swanson old Hollywood look. She and her lawyer would drag me into court to face the same judge who had never liked me from day one. She'd plead for more money and get it, too! It got so bad that I just stopped going to court. I would send my lawyer and pay whatever the judge demanded, God rest his soul. The worst part of this unbelievable story is that my kids were living with me in California and attending school there while I paid my ex-wife for child support in Detroit. Whenever my lawyer mentioned it, the judge's reply was always the same; "That's his problem."

We're gonna fast forward for a moment; you'll get a kick out of this. After my sons finished high school--they were 18 and ready to enter college and their mother talked them into returning to Detroit. She wanted the boys to go to college in Detroit where she lived. She wanted more money. Transformed by one of her disguises, she and her lawyer went back to court - back to the same judge we'd had for the divorce. To everyone's surprise, we learned that this was the judge's last year. The old boy was retiring from the bench. He looked down at her, dressed in her Sad Sack get-up, her new Caddy parked outside. "Don't you think you've fleeced this man long enough?" he said to her and her lawyer. The old man answered his own question; this time he denied her request and threw the plaintiff and her lawyer out of the courtroom! From that day on, I didn't have to pay her another penny! After all these years, the judge's conscience must have been bothering him. May God rest his soul. I heard the case of Stevenson versus Stevenson is in the law books in the state of Michigan. See, there is a God and he's good, too.

As for Elaine, (Ginger Snaps) the mother of my other two sons, I got her a job as a record promoter. She ended up working for three labels at the same time and making good money, too. I made a vow early in life that none of my kids would ever need a handout from anybody. I helped bring them into this world, and it was my responsibility to take care of them, and that's exactly what I did!

Right after I resigned from Motown, I had calls from record companies all over the place wanting me to run their A&R departments. The only call that meant anything was the call from Quincy Jones, who was with Mercury Records at the time. He offered me an A&R job, but I didn't wanna do that anymore unless I was working for myself. "Q" was one of the few people who understood that. I found out later that he was making the same move.

The meeting with Clive Davis at Columbia Records was very interesting, to say the least. We had dinner in his meeting room with his chef, white jacket and all. It was very impressive. That same evening, he invited me to go with him to a theater to see Sylvester, an artist Clive was thinking about signing. We had limousine service, door-to-door, the works. The following day, he offered me a deal to start a label like Motown. The conversation started off well. In fact, it was very exciting until we got down to the money. The amount he offered me to start the label was simply not enough. At that time, Clive had no idea how much money the producers were making at Motown. Either that or he didn't wanna pay me what I needed to make it happen. Some of the producers at Motown were making more every six months than what he was offering me to run a record company. I thanked Clive Davis for the wonderful dinner and the offer, but no thanks! I gotta tell ya that Clive Davis was a class act then, and he's still a class act today. Like Berry Gordy, he's also one of the privileged few given by God the ears for music and an eye for talent.

Starting your own record company is more than a notion. Everybody wanted me to build them another Motown Records, a cash cow, but nobody acknowledged what it took to make the Motown machine work. They all had some idea that to reproduce another Motown, all you had to do was take Mickey Stevenson, have him pluck some Black artists out of the churches, the ghetto or wherever they thought they came from, find some writers, producers, and make it happen. What a joke!

Motown was Berry Gordy's dream, which is the American dream with a twist.

We had to get past the great white dragon spewing white hot fire from its mouth, hell-bent on stopping this Motown American dream from happening. Guess what, dragon? It didn't work.

Motown only grew stronger and the dream got bigger, not because of some secret formula hidden in the studio, not even on the merits of the chairman, who was a great leader. Motown could not be shaken or stirred by outside forces because the individual minds in the company were chosen - that's right, I said chosen--to focus on one thing; creating music together.

The motivation was a Godly one. It's called love.

The Godly creative force of love can take the fire right out of any dragon's mouth, and it did! That's what made Motown a company like no other.

And the hits just kept on coming.

A NEW START

Let's get back to my dilemma.

I had had it up to my neck with this prejudiced record company business. I decided to give it a break for a while. I produced a couple of stage shows for different organizations, and it was during one of the productions for Jesse Jackson that I met Sidney Poitier and Clarence Avant.

I had heard about Clarence as an entrepreneur in the entertainment business, but I never met the man until the evening of the Jackson production. Clarence obviously knew a lot about me. I thought it would be wise to find out as much as I could about him as well. After a few meetings with him, I found that learning about him wasn't very hard because he loved to talk about himself and his accomplishments. Believe me - he had some great accomplishments to talk about. Clarence was a prodigy of Joe Glaser. Joe ran the Associated Booking Corporation back in the day.

I think it was Mahalia Jackson who said, "ABC booking agency was one of the few agencies that Black artists could get some decent work and get your money, honey." It handled artists like Diana Washington, Brook Benton, Sarah Vaughn, Dorothy Dandridge and Billie Holiday, as well as Kitty "Brown Gal" Stevenson. As you can see, this was back in the day.

Through Joe Glaser, Clarence Avant was introduced to plenty of important people in the entertainment industry, and when the right opportunities presented themselves, he took advantage of them. Clarence was one of the few Blacks the white boys in control of the recording industry trusted. When Clarence discovered I was no longer with Motown, he asked me if I would like to have my own label, with him as a partner.

I thought about it very seriously. I realized that going through all the corporate bullshit invariably ate up creative time, time that I needed to build my own record family. But if I partnered with Clarence, who loved handling the corporate stuff, I would be free to do my thing. In the meantime, I could learn more about corporate politics first hand from Clarence. Sounded like a good arrangement to me! Clarence Avant unequivocally had the hook-up. He walked me right into MGM Records to meet Mort Nasatir, the president, and it was as if they had been waiting for me. MGM records cut a deal with us for the new label, sealing one of the first joint venture deals between an African American and a major record company. I thought it would be appropriate to name the label "Venture Records."

It was on! Just like that. There was one thing, however. I had to sign Kim Weston to MGM Records. Why wouldn't they want to kick off the new Venture label with a known artist like Kim? I asked Clarence, whose answer was simple; they want her on MGM, and that's what they want. It made no sense to me, but what the hell! We got Venture Records and MGM got Kim Weston. The deal started out fine. Clarence was doing his corporate thing with MGM and keeping me informed. MGM built me a studio, set up our offices in Beverly Hills and furnished it lavishly; they did the whole nine yards. I told Clarence what I needed, Clarence told MGM what he wanted and they supplied it.

I gotta tell ya, my partner Clarence was a piece of work. I was out in Compton and down in the ghettos of Los Angeles, looking and finding young gifted artists, the hungry talented ones, singers, writers and producers who were willing to work themselves out of the stranglehold of ghetto life. I was putting a good team together; we were on a roll.

But things begin to change. MGM started sending me a cartload of would-be artists to produce, artists signed to their other labels. They all sounded like rejects from American Idol. I turned them down, every one of them, except for the Righteous Brothers. They were known as the blue-eyed soul brothers, and they were very soulful. I had fun producing them. We had a hit on both sides of their record.

Somehow I felt my partner really wanted to be another Berry Gordy, but so did a lot of other guys, so he was in good company. Berry was a great role model. The only problem with that is, there could only be one Berry Gordy, one Mickey Stevenson, one Clarence Avant, and one Motown, for that matter.

The array of talented people who came together in the relentless pursuit to build Motown was a once in a lifetime thing. Motown was the quintessential blueprint for how one can develop artists, writers, producers, everyone needed to create a new force in music. And it was all orchestrated by God. Berry Gordy's dream was the instrument He used to accomplish this. Like everything else God has put His hand to since the beginning of time, this new force was meant to be around forever.

The good thing was that we were all given the formula to follow. It was easy to see that with Clarence and I working together and a wealth of experience and knowledge between us, the ability to follow the formula in time would result in a great company of our own. I did my best to explain this to my partner and to the executives at MGM, but no one was listening. In the meantime, Harry Belafonte, who loved Kim Weston's voice and her patriotic attitude, put her in his show as his opening act.

Belafonte was a perfectionist when it came to entertaining an audience. He knew the theater; he knew how to get the best sound, the best way to use the lights, and where to place his voice. The man was incredible. He was a master at controlling his audience. I learned a lot about theater production just watching him. Backstage and onstage, singing or acting, Harry Belafonte was the man.

He also knew many very rich and influential people. I found out through him that someone was buying up all the stock at MGM. They wanted to take control so they could sell off the record division and build a casino in Las Vegas, the MGM Grand.

When I heard that I knew there was no way for my company, Venture Records, to succeed. My deal had been doomed from the start. MGM Records was folding, and I was supposed to be its saving grace. They wanted me to fly in like Superman, build them another Motown Records, a cash cow! And in a hurry. The words "patience" and "planning" were never in the picture. This was my first lesson in the big game of corporate politics, a game where people's lives, talent and futures meant absolutely nothing; it was all about the bucks, baby.

What a world. This was a world where loyalty, trust and honesty were not important. The entertainment business can be a cold, calculating business that's only interested in using whomever to get whatever, and if people get hurt or even destroyed in the process, so be it.

I say this to all the creators and the talented ones who want to be in this industry and who are lucky enough to read this book. This entertainment trip we're all on can be very rewarding, but you better watch your back!

More and more often, my payroll checks were coming late. I used that as my reason to go to New York and meet with the president of MGM Records again. It was a six-hour flight from L.A. to New York in those days. I had plenty of time to figure out just what to say. I wanted outta this deal. When I walked into the president's office, he immediately started explaining the reason my payroll checks were so late. The excuse was that MGM was going through some reorganizing. Reorganizing, my ass!

The moment he handed me that line of bullshit, I could tell right away Mort knew what was really going on with the infrastructure of MGM. The record division was being abolished. Phased out! I also knew that he had bigger problems than I did; he was going to be out of a job real soon.

"I don't care whose fault it is," I said. "All I know is I'm not getting the support I was promised. This deal is not working. I want out."

A strange thing happened. Mort looked at me with an earnest but sad look on his face, like he didn't know how to say what he wanted to say. After taking a moment and a deep breath, Mort asked me not to leave the company right away. He explained to me that if I resigned right then, it would not look good for him. He would be grateful if I could just hang in there a little longer.

"How much longer is a little while longer?" I asked.

"A couple of months at the most, that's all I need." He replied.

The way he said it made me feel like he really needed my help. While he was talking, I was thinking. Man! To go from president of a company to unemployed, just like that! Wow! This corporate stuff is as cold as ice.

His wife lived in London or was from London. Either way, he was going to London for a few weeks to work something out. I really didn't wanna know all the details. He looked like he had enough troubles without pouring his heart out to me. I said I would hang in there as long as possible. After all, he did make the deal with me, and it was not his fault that the record division was being sold right out from under him. We agreed that, in the meantime, my payroll would continue without any more problems.

"Right?"

"Right!"

As soon as I got back to L.A., I told Clarence I was leaving, that I had it with this deal. I told all the artists and producers that I was giving notice, and that I would release them from their contracts before I left. I didn't tell them why, but I did advise them that it would not be in their best interest to stay under contract without me being there.

Everybody said, "Let me out now!"

And I did.

After a few months, MGM records went under. The president worked out his problems and moved to London. Clarence Avant went on to do greater things, and as for me; after a few legal words back and forth with the MGM lawyers, they finally accepted my resignation. I retained the recording studio and all the unreleased tapes and masters. They also gave me Kim Weston's contract. Do you remember that biological clock that Kim had ticking away? Right after I resigned, I stopped her clock. We got married!

This corporate world, I was finding out, is another animal altogether. I knew I had a lot more to learn, so I decided to stay in L.A. and start my own production and recording studio business. I had some good studio clients, like Ike and Tina Turner, who would book the studio for weeks at a time.

Tina was something to watch, and when she stood in front of that mic, she would give every song all she had. I recorded a number of musical scores for movies and TV with some of the greatest arrangers and musicians in the world, people like Luc Dejesus, Melba Liston, Marty Pach, Richard Henn, and others. While working with them, I learned a lot about film and TV scoring. Hey! I even earned an Academy Award nomination for best score and the title song to the 1969 Hall Bartlett movie, "Changes."

Right about here I have a confession to make. I finally got the opportunity to record an album. You read it right, I cut an album.

I didn't plan on it; come on now, even I know I'm not the best singer in the world. Berry Gordy told me that, years ago. Nevertheless, I cut an album. Let me tell you how it happened before you start forming your own opinion.

Jeff Kruger from London wanted me to produce an album on a gorgeous young Canadian-born actress, Linda Thornson. Linda was one of the stars of the hit TV show, "The Avengers." You remember that show, where the star could throw his derby around and catch the bad guys?

Now, Linda was a wonderful actress, but like me, she was not the greatest singer in the world. As the producer, I did it the Motown way. First, I recorded the track then I sang the song on tape for the artist to study.

The tape would help them find the best way to approach the melody. This method was not meant for every artist, but with some artists it was necessary, you got it? Good!

Now when Jeff heard me singing on the tape, he called me and asked if I ever thought about recording an album, and that I had a good voice. Jeff went on to say that he would love to record me. I want you to notice that Jeff said he would love to record me! At this point I was quite flattered, but I still turned him down. Then he offered me a bundle of money to record the album.

"How much?" I asked, not sure I'd heard him right.

He repeated it.

I could not refuse that offer.

I recorded the album, titled, Here I Am.

It's good. Look it up if you don't believe me! It's my one and only album.

I admit, it was not a big hit album but nevertheless, Berry Gordy, Jr. - eat your heart out!

ALL IS FAIR IN LOVE

I was very busy building my new company, working with writers, artists, producers, you know the drill. My wife, Kim Weston, who had a hit on the ill-fated MGM label, was busy, too - busy driving me crazy about her career and what I was going to do about it.

Al Bell, who was a Kim Weston fan, was after me to sign her to his Stax Records label from the day she left Motown. Now Kim was a Black activist and Southern gal at heart. Her adaptation of the Black national anthem, Lift Every Voice and Sing, was being played on all the Black radio stations across America. Al and Kim would talk for hours about the Black movement rising in the South. Kim had her eye on Stax Records, which was in Memphis, Tennessee. She couldn't wait.

I signed Kim to my friend Al, at Stax Records. Kim cut a new album with Stax and went out on tour, promoting the album and making political speeches. Things were back on track. At least that's what I thought.

Out of the blue, Kim started giving me problems about not spending enough time with her. What is she talking about? I thought. I never did spend much so-called time with her when we were at Motown. She knew that! So why would I have more time for her now that I'm working for myself? I don't get it!

Maybe she thought being married was supposed to change things. Well, guess what? Things did start to change.

It started when I found this very talented young singer, writer, and piano player. He was also tall and handsome. I had no trouble signing him to a record label.

We put out a hot single record, with an album on the way. My girls group, Hodges, James, and Smith, had an album on London Records as well, and it was selling.

Now I get this bright Motown-like idea of putting all of my artists on tour together. I was so excited about the idea that I completely forgot about this "personal time" problem I had with my wife, Kim.

I went to work booking the dates, putting the band together, the whole nine yards. I was on a roll. Now, with all the knowledge I had learned in the streets, I should have been aware that when you put a handsome, six foot tall young man together with an older but attractive female who has some lonely marital problems, and you have them singing duet love songs; that's a classic stupid setup!

It's like a woman letting her promiscuous girlfriend hang around her freaky boyfriend, thinking nothing is gonna happen. You get the picture. In short order, Kim and the young man fell madly in love, or in lust, whatever. All I know is they were madly into something. Everybody knew about them except me. I was too busy promoting records, making deals, and writing musical plays. The musical plays we'll get to later. Right now let's finish this love saga I helped write.

The whole thing blew up in my face while we were on tour. We were in Detroit, my hometown, where I had booked the show in one of the hottest nightclubs in the city. I had grown up with some of the guys who owned the club. The money was great, and they paid me in cash, all up front, too. It was a personal thing, okay? The boys wanted to impress me. They wanted me to know they had made it and they were handling some big paper. (That means cash money.)

It happened like this –

I was in the basement of the club playing poker with the boys while my artists were up onstage performing. We were having a hell of a time; I hadn't seen the boys in years. We were all friends back in the day, hustling, trying to survive, and now they had their own nightclub, and were rolling in paper. They couldn't wait for me to show up so they could show off. Here I was, winning big at the poker table, high as I could be, and we were all having big fun.

Kim and my handsome young star were upstairs onstage, singing the roof off. I still remember the song they were singing when all hell broke loose. It was Close To You, by the Carpenters. You remember that one: Just like me, they long to be, close to you."

Everybody at the poker table was saying, "Man! They are wearing that song out. You should record them on that song. We never heard it like that before. They are putting some soul into that song! That's a hit!"

At that moment, one of the boys came running downstairs, shouting,

"Hey! You guys gotta see this! Mickey's woman and that young guy she's singing with, they're onstage crying their eyes out and singing up a storm!"

All of a sudden, the music stopped and we heard a lot of noise. The ceiling began to rumble and shake from the ruckus being made by the people upstairs. They were running out of the building as if something or someone was on fire.

Someone started shouting from the stairway, "Hey, Mickey, your piano player has locked himself in a car! He's holding a gun to his head! He's talking about committing suicide, right now, man! Kim is all over the car crying like a baby. Mickey! You better get up here, man the whole club is outside going crazy!"

I was in shock, hearing all this crazy stuff going on.

To make matters worse, the boys who owned this club were not the cleanest guys in town, you know what I mean? They started getting sober real quick, running around cleaning up the place, hiding stuff everywhere.

One of the boys turned to me and said, "I don't want the cops coming down on me, man, 'cause if they come down on me, then we gotta come down on you. You see what I'm saying? This show belongs to you, now you get up there and clean this shit up before it gets outta hand, Mickey, and make it quick, bro, you know what I mean?"

I knew exactly what he meant. He meant my ass was on the line. I acted real calm. "Don't worry, I'll handle it." As I started up the stairs, he said, "I ain't worried, man, but I think you better be."

By the time I reached the parking lot I had to fight my way through the crowd. Sure enough, there they were.

The piano player was locked in the car with a gun to his head, crying like a baby. Kim had her face pressed up against the car window, tears and mascara running down her face and onto the window.

"Oh baby, put the gun down!" she sobbed. "Don't do it! Please don't do it!" Then she saw me. Her face was wet with runny makeup mixed with tears. "We want to be together," she told me. "We love each other. Please, you gotta let us be together."

I looked over at the boys standing there with their arms folded. They were giving me that "You better hurry up" look. I had no choice.

"You two can be together; it's okay!" I said. "Now please tell him to put the gun down, and get out of the car. You can have each other. I mean it, I swear!"

The young boy, who was still holding the gun to his head, shouted, "I don't believe you! I'm not coming out until you leave us! Leave us now!" He cocked the gun like he was ready to fire it.

Now, personally, I didn't think he was gonna do anything. And if we'd been anyplace else, I would have told him "Go ahead and kill your fool self."

But the boys were looking at me, to see what I was going to do. Whatever it was, they wanted me to hurry up and do it before the cops got there. I started walking away, "Look, Kim. I'm leaving. I'm leaving right now!"

I hurried to my car. As I was pulling out of the parking lot, one of the boys came over to me and said, "Hey Mickey, we appreciate the way you handled this thing, man. I know how you must feel too, bro, I really do." He leaned in the car window and very calmly said, "About the show, you know everybody has to stay here and finish this gig, bro. We paid you cash money for three days. You see what I'm saying? Now they got two more days to go. We're not gonna have a problem with this, are we?"

"Problem?" I said, "What problem? I'm outta here. You call me later and tell me how everything went." I gave him the high five and drove off.

You have no idea how bad I felt. I had to leave my wife and her young lover at the club, singing love songs for two more days, while they fell deeper and deeper in love with each other. Not to mention the fact that I had to kiss all that sweet easy poker money good-bye. I was crushed, hurt, upset, pissed off, and everything else you could think of.

I went straight to the hotel, packed my bags and took a flight to Miami Beach. I stayed at the Fontainebleau Hotel, where my man Sammy Davis, Jr. was performing. Sammy and I had a great time while he helped me heal my broken heart. Oh yeah! My heart was broken, I'm not gonna lie about that. I tried to play it off, but it's not easy to do when your woman is telling you, to your face, that another man makes her feel good.

Now that is a real ego crusher. And you can quote me on that. It hurt!

The boys in Detroit called me while I was in Miami. They told me the show was great! And with all the hullabaloo that went on between Kim and the boyfriend, they had to hold the show over for two more days. They thanked me for handling everything so well, and sent me a nice piece of money for the extra shows.

The two lovers decided to stay in Detroit and live together. I went back to L.A. and got busy working on my plays. If you're wondering what happened to the two lovebirds, it wasn't long before they fell out of love, or rather he fell out of lust.

He was too young and broke, and with me outta the picture, she didn't have enough money to keep him from looking at all those fine, young, short-skirt, tight-jean-wearing shapely girls his own age. You see what I'm saying? Sooner or later we all learn that romance without finance can be a nuisance.

As for me managing them, I dropped them both like hot potatoes.

Well, can you blame me? That's better than me killing somebody, don't you agree?

This way I would be killing them softly. Just kidding!

I know you find it hard to believe that I really had a broken heart. Well, I did! I'm human like you. It's probably harder for you to imagine Mickey Stevenson trying to mend his broken heart, right?

Try this on for size. I went all the way to London just to try and shake my friend Mr. Heartache. While in London I hooked up with my friend Johnny Nash. You remember Johnny Nash and his worldwide hit, I Can See Clearly Now? What a great song. Music can be very comforting, and the lyrics to that song were right on time for me. Johnny was on tour in England, so his manager Danny Sims asked me to come along and help Johnny with his live show. What a good idea! I thought; this was just what I needed to help me lose the blues.

While on tour, I met Bob Marley and the Wailers. It helped me lose the heartache and gain some new friends. Johnny reminded me of my brother, Marvin Gaye; talented, creative, and very vulnerable. They were absolutely alike, the way they wore their emotions on their sleeves. You could hear it in the music; you could even see the emotion on Johnny's face - a face that never seemed to age. Like Dorian Gray, the trouble was in the heart. I was not at all surprised when Johnny Nash called it quits. He just walked away from the music world. Johnny got a ranch in Texas and is doin' fine. It was like he connected spiritually with himself. And that's a good thing.

WILLIAM R.

As soon as I got back to L.A., I got a phone call from Marvin Gaye. He wanted me to come over to his studio right away. "I'm in trouble, William R.," he said.

"Marvin, where are you?"

"I'm in my studio. Come over man, okay?"

I hadn't heard from him in a long time, but I could still recognize the sound in his voice when he had a problem. His voice had a lot of stress in it, so I didn't waste any time getting to his studio. That Motown family feeling of love for each other was always there, and for me it will always be there.

When I walked into the control room, Marvin's assistant said, "Are you William R.? Man, am I glad you're here. Marvin's in the studio."

As I opened the door to the studio, I could see him slumped over the piano, his hands on the keys. He was dressed in a white suit, with his shirt opened, and his tie pulled halfway down. He looked like he had just come offstage. I knew right away he was out of it. The studio was full of musicians sitting around waiting while the clock was running. This was a union session, and it had gone into overtime. These musicians were taking advantage of my brother Marvin, who was in no condition to continue a recording session. They all knew it, and they could tell I didn't like what I saw.

The first thing I did was stop the clock. I told everybody, "That's it! It's over. You'll all get paid, now get outta here." One of the musicians, a friend of mine, helped me carry Marvin up to the loft in the studio, where he could get some rest.

On the way up the stairs, Marvin looked at me with heavy, tearful eyes and said,

"Thank you, William R. I didn't know what to do, man, all I could think about was calling you like we used to do at Motown."

"You did the right thing, my brother," I said as we laid him down on the couch. "Everything's under control. Now get some rest."

Marvin passed out the moment his head hit the pillow. He had a peaceful look on his face - as if he was happy he could finally get some sleep.

It felt good knowing that I could help him, even though I knew it would only be temporary. I stayed there for a while to make sure he was okay.

You see, my brother Marvin was in trouble. All the so-called friends, the parties, sex and drugs were only a temporary solution, a quick fix, as we say. As I sat there looking at him, I could still see how vulnerable he was. I guess it comes with the territory, you know what I mean? Being creative and being vulnerable go together like a hand and glove, and that's a fact!

I didn't hear from Marvin for a long time after that. Then, out of nowhere, I got a call from some folks at the record company. They wanted some liner notes from me. It turns out Marvin had used some of the songs that he and I had written, in an album that was being released soon.

I laughed to myself. I knew that was Marv's way of saying, "Thank you, William R., thank you."

And the hits just kept on coming.

VANESSA

My friend Redd Foxx, the comedian and star of the TV show, "Sanford and Son," had just opened his beauty and barber salon on the famous Sunset Boulevard in Hollywood, CA. That was a big thing in those days. This was the first time ever that a Black man had anything like that on Sunset Boulevard, and on the strip, too! That was really a no-no!

Redd Foxx had the shop laid out with palm trees and flowers inside and out. There were beautiful girls to serve you wine, coffee, whatever. It was fabulous. Black people visiting L.A. from all over the world made it a point to have something done to their hair or nails at the Redd Foxx salon on Sunset Boulevard.

I had just had my hair fixed and was under the dryer, asleep as always, when I opened my eyes and saw a beautiful, petite girl in a pair of hip-hugging jeans, staring at me. I thought I was dreaming. I could tell she knew who I was. After I pulled myself together, I asked the hostess, who was my barber, "Who is that?"

My barber whispered in my ear. "Her name is Vanessa from North Carolina," she said, "and she was asking about you, too. But don't worry about a thing. I told her all the good stuff about you, okay? So you can take it from here."

I thanked her with a twenty-dollar bill. As she wrapped it around a wad of her tips, she smiled and said, "You're something else."

You know how it is when you see someone who really turns you on and you can tell the feeling is mutual? We were just looking each other over, imagining all the good things we could do to one another, all those electrifying Oh! My God! kinda' things. Well, that's what happened. We fell in lust with each other immediately.

By the time real love came into this picture, Vanessa was back home in North Carolina, good and pregnant.

It was during the Christmas holiday and I was on my way to meet her folks in Greensboro, N.C., to give them the good news. Her father picked me up at the airport and I could tell right away that he was one of those half-rich bougie Negroes of Greensboro.

We were still called Negroes then, back in the day. The word "Blacks" was just beginning to work its way in. The father had no love at all for people in show business and had no problem telling me so. He talked all the way to the house, giving me his opinion about artists and how lazy show business people are. After about ten minutes of his insulting remarks, I just tuned him out. I was too busy taking in Greensboro's beautiful picture postcard scenery. The winter snow covering the treetops made for a breathtaking backdrop. As a city boy, I had never seen anything like it.

When we reached the house with its big picture windows and Vanessa standing at the door waving at me, man! It was like a vision only seen in the movies. I fell in love with the whole scene right then and there. We pulled into the carport, where there were two other matching cars, the mother's and Vanessa's. I thought I was in another world. This was as good as it gets.

Right after dinner, her father told me he would be taking me to a hotel. Vanessa's mother said, "Why can't he stay here? We have plenty of room."

Her father frowned. "He's going to the hotel."

Vanessa spoke up, very softly but directly. "Daddy, if he goes to the hotel, I'm going with him. Do you understand that?"

All of a sudden, daddy turned into another person. "Oh no, Vanessa, he can stay here if that's what you want. Your mother will fix up the guest room."

That's how I found out Vanessa was not only a daddy's girl, she was in charge. I felt sorry for her mother, but I guess she had become used to the two of them over the years.

The following day, Vanessa told her parents she was pregnant. Her mother was very happy for her, but her father, man, was he upset! He told her she could not have that baby in their home town. He was concerned about his neighbors and his image. They started to argue and talking crazy to each other. This was getting too deep for me. The beautiful picture postcard of Greensboro, N.C., fell apart. It was back to reality.

Her father hated the idea that his precious little Vanessa was pregnant, and by someone in the lazy entertainment business. O my God! That was disgusting. As for Vanessa moving to L.A. with me, to have the baby, that was out of the question.

Where could she go? Vanessa didn't like being too far away from her parents. So they decided she would move to Baltimore, open a beauty shop, and have the baby there. Vanessa knew the hair business very well. She'd learned it from her mother, who was one of the leading beauticians in Greensboro. I went along with this saga.

I bought her a shop in Baltimore with all the trimmings. She had an apartment, a housekeeper - the works. I flew back and forth from L.A. to Baltimore every other week. The week after my daughter, Ashley Stevenson, was born, I flew into Baltimore. To my surprise, I found the beauty shop had been sold. When I got to the apartment, it was empty. Vanessa and my baby were gone, baby clothes and all. I found myself standing in the middle of an empty apartment reading a letter addressed to me.

"I'm going back home with my daddy," the letter said. "He came and got me. He's been very unhappy without me, Mickey, and I can't let that happen to him. My daddy is old and he needs me very much. Mickey I love you, but you have your music business to keep you happy. My daddy only has me. Don't worry about your daughter, Ashley. She'll be fine." That was it. No good-bye, no nothing, just gone. Talk about being in shock, man! I took the next flight to Greensboro, only to hear her tell me the same thing to my face.

She was staying home with her father, and my daughter Ashley would be fine. There was nothing left for me to say. Her father offered to drive me back to the airport. I didn't like that idea but what the hell; it was over.

When we arrived at the airport, I met two of his friends. They were cops - I mean big white cowboy hat-wearing cops, right outta the Wild West, guns hanging off their hips and all. The only thing missing was the horse. They were waiting for me.

They advised me not to return to Greensboro any time soon. After looking them over, I took their advice under serious consideration. Guess what? I left and I did not return.

It wasn't until after the old man passed on that I got a chance to spend time with my beautiful daughter Ashley, but that's another story.

MOTOWN EVOLUTION

By this time, Motown had gone through quite a few changes as well. Holland- Dozier-Holland, the great hit-makers of Motown's hottest artists, left the family, as I knew they would. Jeffrey Bowen took over the A&R department after they left, and he was even worse. He had no talent at all - no feel for the artists or the musicians. In other words, he didn't have a clue. The only thing he had going for him was that he loved Motown. How do I know all this about Jeffrey? He had worked for me first, and I knew him well.

Eddie Holland took the team of Holland-Dozier-Holland to one of the major labels and got a distribution deal. They started their own record company, Invictus Records. They made some good records; one with Freda Payne, Band of Gold, among others. The Invictus promotion and sales force did not compare to Barney Ales' magnificent seven at Motown, though, and consequently, Invictus folded.

Marvin Gaye also left the Motown family after running into all kinds of personal problems, legal problems, management problems and God knows what else. In my opinion, the spiritual side of Marvin was also a problem for him; he knew it and so did I. You see we talked about it from the day we met. Sometimes he would try to redirect this spiritual energy into his songs or he'd choose other ways like the rest of us who chose to give into worldly desires; games, fast cars, sex, even drugs entered the picture. Hey, you know what I'm talking about nobody's innocent or without sin, especially in this business. But the gift of the spirit was embedded in Marvin, and even though he tried to lose it, it never left him.

When faced with a host of problems, including spiritual struggles, a creative and deeply sensitive talent like Marvin Gaye will shut down or find other ways to avoid the problems. It's my opinion and I believed that in Marvin's case, he did them both. Marvin stayed away from the business and America for quite some time, using the time and space to find himself and to accept his spiritual connection and the peace that comes with it.

Marvin pulled himself together. When he resurfaced, he went over to Columbia Records, by way of Larkin Arnold. Larkin was the legal eagle for Black artists at the label, and he was very much in tune with their problems. Larkin was not like most Black attorneys, the ones who turned white on you the moment they got a position with a major company. Larkin believed in Marvin and went to bat for him.

Marvin was more determined than ever to make a comeback. Once again, when total focus and relentless pursuit to be the best come into play, success is inevitable. Marvin came up with some great songs and was back on top bigger than ever!

From 1962 until he went to be with the Lord, Marvin always knew that wherever he was, he could count on me. Marvin knew I had his interest at heart at all times. It was a spiritual thing.

The Motown family feeling was slipping away. Even though new artists were being signed, the feeling of love and pride that had originated among the artists, the writers, the producers, even the musicians and staff, was slowly being pushed aside. Motown was turning into a record company like all the others.

Don't get me wrong. The Motown sound machine was moving along and going strong. The standards for artists being signed to Motown were set in brick. As the A&R man for Motown, I had set that standard high and it was holding. New artists like Rick James, the Commodores, Lionel Richie, The Jackson 5, Edwin Starr, Teena Marie, Ashford and Simpson - and I'm sure I left out a few - were all wonderful.

My point is that even though the hits just kept on coming, the love was fading away. Ashford and Simpson's production on Diana Ross was an inspiration. Lionel Richie's songs were outstanding and added more fuel to the Motown string of hits. There were many talented people at Motown doing their thing, turning out some great records, but they were working as individuals, most definitely not as a family.

The name Motown was the tie that connected them - but the heart and soul of Motown was slipping away. By the time the Jackson 5, who were hot on Motown, stopped scrambling around, they ended up on the Sony label as the Jacksons, not the Jackson 5. You see, the name Jackson 5 belonged to Motown, if my memory serves me correctly. Jermaine Jackson, who was married to Berry's daughter, stayed with his father-in-law's company, while the rest of the boys went to Sony with Michael singing the lead.

Personally, I liked the sound of the Jackson 5. That's when the two leads, Jermaine and Michael, carried the songs. After three or four albums as The Jacksons - and like 90 percent of the lead singers in groups - Michael ended up going it alone.

Even Diana Ross went to another company. Motown changed presidents a few times, along with producers, writers, even A&R directors - the works. The face of Motown was definitely evolving. God bless the millions upon millions of fans who heard the music of Motown and fell in love with the artists and their songs.

It's their love and admiration for the original Motown Sound that keeps this music alive and still going strong. Wow! That's awesome.

And the hits just keep on coming.

MOTOWN 25

The Motown 25 was a moment to remember. It was one of the greatest TV productions in the history of American music. Not just for America but for music lovers around the world. Only the chairman, Berry Gordy, Jr., could have reached out and called all the artists, writers, producers, even the staff of the original Motown family back together for this reunion. No matter what labels or companies they were with, they all came back to the place that showed them the love, to be part of Motown 25. Everyone who'd touched the dream or had been part of the dream - all came together for this memorable reunion.

The Motown 25 show was fantastic! The video was off the hook; even to this day they still talk about how unbelievable it was. Marvin Gaye laid it on the line with What's Goin' On, and Michael Jackson's Billie Jean was electrifying. The Four Tops and The Temptations' duel in the sun dazzled the audience. Of course, the diva Diana Ross, who never fails to wrap an audience around her finger, did just that. Richard Pryor, like Dick Clark and so many others, gave it their all. The piano scene with the producers, Holland-Dozier-Holland, Harvey Fuqua, Ron Miller and Me all singing the company song and describing how we made the hits, was something to see. But the most astonishing thing was the respect and admiration that they all still had for me. Man after all those years, that was an amazing feeling. You really could feel the love, respect and honor in the tremendous standing ovation given to the chairman, after Smokey made his speech. Yeah! The Motown 25 was an affirmation to all of us that the dream was alive and doing well. The Motown 25 DVD sold like a hit record, and all the other Motown products started selling as well, and are still selling.

And the hits just keep on coming.

THE CHAIRMAN LETS
MOTOWN GO

It was inevitable.

One day I got the news that Motown Records had been sold to Universal, one of the big conglomerates. For a moment it brought tears to my eyes. It's not that I didn't know that someday, Berry was gonna sell the company. I just didn't know how much it would affect me. I gotta tell ya, it was as if I had just lost a member of my family, as if someone I loved very much had passed on. I must have had a hundred calls from people all over asking me, "Why did B.G. sell Motown?" "Why did he sell it so cheap? He should have held on to it." "He should have held out for more money."

There were so many questions and opinions from the would-be geniuses out there that I just stopped listening. Since you've read the book up to this point, you're either a Motown fan, or a music fan, or maybe you just wanna know. So let's shed some light on this subject. Stay with me, now!

B.G. sold Motown Records to Universal Records, but he held on to Jobete Music, the publishing company. Now it takes the artist plus the song to make a hit record. You can't have one without the other. Are you still with me? Good! In order for Universal Records to make its money back plus a profit, it would have to package and repackage the product, market it, promote it, sell and resell the Motown catalog.

For a few years, Motown Records division (under Universal) had been searching within the conglomerate world of music executives for a leader to run the Motown Records division. Everyone they found would only have moderate periods of success, and they would soon be replaced with another hopeful leader. This went on for a while. In my humble opinion, I believe they found who and what they need in Ethiopia Habtemariam. Like Berry Gordy and Clive Davis, she's patient, relentless and she has the gift. Like I said, that's just my opinion.

And the hits just keep on coming.

LOVE LIFE & MORE

"You better treat 'em right;
Karma has no expiration date."

I would like to explain something right here and now. I'm really a very romantic person at heart. I really am. I love being in love, can't you see that? Love is all through my book, and I have the kids to prove it. You see what I'm sayin'?

Guess what? I want you to know that I would love to have met a woman who really understood me, someone who accepted me for who I am.

This is no reflection on all the women who were in my life. I'm sure they must've loved or tried to accept me for me, at one time - at least I hope they did. If not, that's okay! You see, I learned something.

After the first woman kicked me to the curb (as you know, that first kick always hurts the most, and takes the longest time to get over), I learned that you must press past the pain of change, in order to survive.

I made up my mind that if it ever happens again, I won't be throwing myself a pity party or doing the Oh my God! Why me? bit. No way! I've learned that all pain goes away...

...even pain of the heart.

Let me give you some examples...

Melanie, Melanie Burke, the girl could lo mo blow (slang for sing her ass off) and had a body built like a brick shipyard. She was the daughter of the Hall of Fame blues singer, Solomon Burke, so you know she could sing. What we have here is the older man and the younger lady story.

It was the Detroit love saga in reverse, only this time I got caught up in the deal. Yep! You got it! I fell for the old okey-doke and ended up spending a mountain of money, and wound up with three more kids; my son Novel, my daughter Mikkia and their sister Amber. I must admit I do have some beautiful kids, and smart, too. At least I did something right!

As the story goes, that relationship didn't last very long, either. You know the ending all too well; younger lady meets young man and dumps the older man. That's the nuts and bolts of it. In case you're trying to figure out how many kids that makes, let me save you the trouble of going back through the book. The answer is seven. OK!

I can't remember just how many of these merry-go-round romances I've been through, with all the women in my life. What I do remember is my success rate has been a disaster. Now I ask you, do I know how to pick 'em or what? Don't you dare answer that!

Now on a flight from Atlanta I met Sandra, a gorgeous young lady with peach-colored skin and big brown eyes that were full of tears. This was her first time on an airplane, and she was scared to death. The girl was holding the armrest so tight she looked like she was frozen to the seat. Being the gentleman that I am, I moved next to her and tried to console her, help take her mind off her misery, so to speak. Before I could say anything to her, the plane made a quick, turbulent drop. She grabbed my hand and started squeezing it and I mean she held on tight. As the plane leveled off, she apologized to me. I gave her my best reassuring smile, "It's okay! I rather enjoyed it." She smiled and began to relax when - Wow! The plane dipped again. This time she grabbed my hand and didn't let go. We talked all the way to L.A. When we landed, she still didn't want to let my hand go. She held on for a few days, which turned into a few weeks. And a few years later, Brian Martin Stevenson was born. (side note: he gets his superior work ethic from me.)

I really loved Sandra and I decided this was it. She understands me, I thought. She's not too demanding, I thought. She'd make a good wife, I thought. I was beginning to be acknowledged as a musical playwright - can you believe that? My shows were receiving nominations and winning NAACP Image Awards. I was on a roll creatively, but my personal life was falling apart again.

It happened right after I got the news that I had won my first Image award for best musical play. I was overwhelmed; it was like winning an Oscar. I rushed home to tell my wife all about it and how happy I felt. I was right in the middle of telling her when out of nowhere, and without a smile on her face, she said, and I quote: "I'm glad for you and your award, but there's something I'd like to say to you. I need some space from you."

Her words stopped me cold. I said, "You need what?"

As I looked into Sandra's eyes, I knew, I could see it and feel it. There was another man in this picture. All those nights I was in the theater working and studying like an insane man, doing my thing; and I must admit I was doing a few other things as well, she was studying hard, too, and doing her thing. Of course she denied it at first, but after the tears and denials eventually came the famous, much-derided "I-don't-know-how-it-happened-I-didn't-intend-for-it-to-go- this-far" bull! The bottom line is she wanted some space from me, to see if Mr. Wonderful was going to make her happy.

Obviously, I wasn't. Hey! It wasn't all her fault. I realize that I can really get wrapped up in my career moves and lose track of time and space. Everybody can't hang with someone who loves what he does as much as I do. And that's the point. This is me, and creating is what I love to do!

Anyway, we made a deal. I would give her all the space she needed, and she would let me see my son (who was three years old at the time) whenever I wanted to. That was fine with her, and it was cool with me! She and Mr. Wonderful moved in together, right down the street from me. Why did they have to move that close? They could've move somewhere else, hell! Anywhere but right down the street from me.

As it turned out, Mr. Wonderful was the insurance salesman who had tried to get me to buy a three million dollar policy. I remember the day she introduced me to him, with his shirt wide open and a heavy gold chain hanging around his neck. I had no intention of buying anything from that brother. Anyway, her little piece of heaven lasted for about six months. It turned out that Mr. Wonderful had two other girlfriends and was living with one. He wasn't after Sandra's love, he was after her money, or should I say after my money! Like I said, that's my opinion and I'm sticking to it!

She got Mr. Wonderful and her permanent space, and I got closer than ever to my son, ten nominations and five awards. To this day, my son and I are inseparable. Sandra and I? We're good friends, too.

Then there was one girl who had it all. Jennie Bell was one of the first Black Playboy bunnies. She was gorgeous, with great eyes, a great body and brains. Jennie was so together she even gave actor Richard Burton trouble. The girl was a real soul shaker and a heart breaker. She had her dreams and the ambition to go after them. With all that equipment, she was unstoppable. We were too much alike for our romance to last. By the way, she's still beautiful and she pulled it off.

217

Look at it like this. Everyone has the right to be happy, right? Well! That includes me. I never understood why a woman would want to leave me in the first place. I've always considered myself the catch of the day, one of the good guys. You see what I'm saying!

Still, it must've been a figment of my imagination because, as you can see, everybody kept kicking me to the curb. The last woman who walked out on me described me as an "unromantic workaholic."

Who, me?

INNER CITY

*"Every successful person
had someone who believed in them."*
~ WMS

It was by accident that I started working with the Inner City Cultural Center in L.A. Cliff Roquemore, the director for the cultural center, was from Detroit and a big Motown fan. He asked me to write some music for one of the productions he was putting on for the center. He told me how the kids would go crazy if someone like me got involved with Inner City.

I went by to see what he was talking about, and it was amazing to see all those kids working together, young talented artists, singers, actors, dancers and writers, all of them hungry and eager to learn.

It was like seeing the Motown energy all over again. They were all so excited about working with the man from Motown. They had no idea how excited I was about them. I did not want to disappoint these kids.

I told Cliff I had never worked on a Broadway show before; I had no idea where or how to start. Clifford said, "You're a natural; all you need to do is work with me. I'll teach you everything you need to know. We'll write the book together." And we did!

Cliff, who was a great director, worked harder than anybody I ever knew. He would work all day at the center with the kids then spend eight to nine hours every night working with me on my scriptwriting. He showed me how to deliver the story without telegraphing the songs, leaving room for the director to create.

After working with film scores and TV production with some of the best arrangers in the world, I was able to incorporate the musical sounds of Motown and show tunes into the framework of a musical play.

This was some of the most productive time I had spent since Motown. Our musical play, Show Girls, was a huge success. It was the biggest thing that had happened at the Cultural Center Theater, ever.

People came from all over the city to see Mickey Stevenson and Cliff Roquemore's, Show Girls. It ran for 21 weeks.

I got better at writing musical plays and I really enjoyed it. I received a call from Valarie Benning, who was with the major theater group in Atlanta. They wanted some original musical plays, and they wanted us to come to Atlanta and produce them. Valarie felt the music of Motown, mixed with the sound of show tunes and based on an original story, was just what Atlanta needed. She made all the arrangements and even helped us mount the production in our first major theater. That was very exciting!

By now you should know how I feel about talented people. Valarie was an extraordinary person, ambitious and talented. She and I hit it off right from the bat. She had a loyalty that I found to be rare in an ambitious woman. Most of the ambitious women in this business will use you just to accomplish their own goals. Valarie was different. She loved my work and had an admiration for me that grew into a loyal friendship. She came from a family of very talented girls. When I met her mother and father, I saw the love between them, and the spiritual connection. What a family!

We had great success with the show in Atlanta. Valarie talked the city into bringing us back for three more years. This helped me improve my writing and casting.

It also gave me an opportunity to put each show on its feet. I learned quickly, and within three years I had written and produced a number of successful shows - Showgirls, Swann, TKO, The Gospel Truth, and Wings & Things.

Where there is loyalty, love and respect in the friendship, it is boundless. I have a love for Valarie, who has been my friend for over 25 years. I truly understand what a true friend is, and how rare it is. Thank you, Valarie, love you baby.

One of the greatest pleasures of my new life in the musical theater was working with Valarie and other extremely talented people, some of whom went on to do great things.

Lynn Whitfield is one. A wonderful actress and singer who played Josephine Baker in my play, Lynn was also chosen to play the great Josephine in a two-hour "Movie of the Week" production. She was magnificent.

Lynn has starred in a number of great movies throughout the years, but I'm personally proud of the Josephine Baker story. I also had the joy of learning from Ernie Hudson and Glynn Turman, two extremely good actors who are all over the screen in feature films and TV, non-stop. Glynn is now directing films.

But my favorite, the one I knew would be a fantastic actor, was Forest Whitaker. When he portrayed the character Snake in my play, Swann, I knew he would be unstoppable. Forest's leading role in the movie, The Crying Game, was remarkable, but his portrayal of Idi Amin in The Last King of Scotland was simply awe-inspiring. I personally thought it was an Academy Award winning performance, and guess what? He received the Academy Award as best actor! Go check it out.

If you recall, I talked about the five essentials: ability, material, charisma, complete focus, and a relentless pursuit to be the best. Are you starting to get a handle on it? Good!

Working with underprivileged kids and young adults in the Inner City Cultural Center was an amazing experience. The kids and everyone there all seemed so appreciative. The look on their faces whenever I spoke to them was a reward in itself. I had never seen such focus and absorption of information before. These kids took every word out of my mouth as though it were some kind of mental nourishment. That kind of admiration can make you humble. I was from Motown, and what it stood for meant the world to them.

This hunger for information made me realize I had to do more, much more. I brought other known artists to the center to talk to them, to answer their questions and let them know it's not magic or luck that helps you get over, it's believing in yourself and going after what you believe in.

We had seminars every other week, and it felt great to be giving something back. To be honest with you, I was the winner, not only because of the wonderful feeling it gave me, but because they were teaching me far more than I could ever teach them. Through them, I learned about theater, actors, directing, lighting, sets - all of it.

I devoted a large part of my time to working with them and loved every minute of it. I found an energizing new career in the world of theater. I finally appreciated what my brother, Lonnie, was feeling in this fascinating theater world; its effect was hypnotic.

While under its spell I fell head over heels into another relationship.

TAYLOR'S MOM - B'ANCA

"That's What Love is All About."

B'anca is an actress/singer who loves the theater. It was at the Inner City Theater that we hooked up.

I was working on some music for a show, and she was working as the assistant director. Not only could she explain his directing to the actors, but if they didn't get it right, she would jump on the stage and act it out for them.

The girl was wonderful, sexy, and cute, too! In some ways, she reminded me of myself, though not the cute, sexy part. Watch it now! I'm talking about the energy she put out. B'anca had that "let's get it on" spirit - nonstop. She had a real superwoman thing goin' on. She also had her son Patrick, and she was trying to raise him by herself. It all drew me in like a magnet. Like the other relationships in my life, this one started out with me helping her. In this case, I gave B'anca a job as my personal secretary. Along with the job, I gave her one of the rooms in my place to share with her son, Patrick. It wasn't long before she became more than my personal secretary. It became strictly personal all the way. Check this out! I remember the first time we made mad, passionate love. She said, "Right after having really great sex with me, you jump up and go write a song, or something. What is that about?"

I explained to her that her love inspired me to create something. Now how poetic is that? I've learned that I shouldn't count on forever, just enjoy each day one day at a time, and leave the rest to God. Through all this creating and producing, B'anca and I managed to create the greatest little daughter in the world. I know because I was in the delivery room from the beginning to the end. B'anca was listening to Michael Bolton sing That's What Love is All About while the doctor was delivering the baby. I was a nervous wreck as I watched the doctor deliver my baby.

Wow! Now that was quite an experience. I hurried and gave B'anca a kiss for going through all that pain, and then I took off down the hall after the nurse who had my baby. I wanted to follow her and watch her put the name "Taylor Stevenson" on the tag, and place it on my baby's little arm.

You see, I had read that these hospitals are known for misplacing a baby or two. Oh no! Not my baby. I named her after my mother, who would have loved her to life.

I think television and the Internet are making kids grow up a lot faster and a whole lot smarter. Have you noticed that, too? The good news is her mother taught my baby to love the Lord. It's He who will help keep her stable as she grows up in an unstable world. I have to admit, my life has been enriched with Taylor in it.

When she was ten and a half years old, going on seventeen, I was totally surprised when I was asked to be the Black History Month guest speaker at an aerospace firm's observance. One of the first Black astronauts also was to be on the program. My daughter asked if she could go with me.

Just before bringing me onstage, the announcer walked out and said "Music, please." One of our old hits, the song *Mickey's Monkey*, began to blast. The announcer started singing and dancing along with the song; he was all over the stage having a good time. You would have thought he was one of The Temptations. Mickey's Monkey had to be his favorite song.

When the song was over and he was practically out of breath, he introduced me. "Ladies and gentleman, I am proud to present to you the writer and producer of some of the world's biggest hit songs ever, like "Dancing in the Street," "It Takes Two," "Devil With the Blue Dress," "Just Ask The Lonely," "My Baby Loves Me." He went on and on: "Pride and Joy," "Stubborn Kind of Fellow." He named songs even I had forgotten I wrote. I kept waving my hand to make him stop, but it didn't work. Not only did he rattle off every song, he named the entire list of artists I brought to Motown. The guy had really done his homework. The buildup was so fantastic I was thinking Wow! Did I do all that? I was too embarrassed to walk onstage.

I heard him say, "Music, please!" And *Mickey's Monkey* revved up again.

"Ladies and gentleman! The original A&R director of Motown Records - William Mickey Stevenson!" I quickly pulled myself together and walked onstage to a standing ovation. More than a thousand people were applauding, and "Mickey's Monkey" was still blasting. When I reached the mic, someone hollered, "We love you and your song, 'Mickey's Monkey!' "

"I love you too!" I shouted back. "But I gotta' tell you. I hate that damn song!"

The whole audience went up in laughter. It was great! I spoke for over an hour, and I left the stage like I entered, with a standing ovation.

I did not write Mickey's Monkey.

It was written and produced by Holland- Dozier-Holland, and recorded by my brother Smokey Robinson and the Miracles. Now the question is; who or what inspired the writers to write Mickey's Monkey? Was it inspired (a) after watching Mickey groom and develop the artist Kim Weston? Or was it inspired (b) after watching Mickey producing, when he's working in the studio?

Let's examine letter (a). Kim Weston would do everything I told her to do, while I was working with her career as an artist. Things like extending her hair, having her clothes made, finding a makeup artist to teach her how to apply day and night time makeup, lining up her shows, picking her songs.

Let's examine letter (b). As you must know by now, I'm the kinda guy who'll get totally engrossed in the studio, really worked up, when I'm producing a track for a song. Working with the Funk Brothers made it even more invigorating. They knew my style, and how I loved music, from jazz to rock and roll and everything in between.

The Funk Brothers and I were on the same page. We had a lot of fun in the studio. From the time I pointed to the drummer to give me a pickup on the drums, the dance was on! I could feel the rhythm all the way down to my toes and I'd start moving. I'd dance over to the bass player for a funky accent, yea! I'd really be feeling it then. I'd get down eye to eye with the guitar players, and while I'd be movin' and groovin' to the beat, I'd be telling them to forget the lead sheets, just to follow me for colors, and give me some soulful fill-ins.

By then I'd be bobbin' and weavin', from the tambourine to the solo lines coming from the piano. Everybody would be into it. All this would be happening while I was dancing to the music. Now back to the question.

What inspired the hit song, Mickey's Monkey?

Answer: Letter (b).

Final answer.

MOTOWN 45

The Motown 45 TV show was a hit idea from the start. I would use the hottest artists of today to sing the Motown songs of yesterday. Combine that with the original Motown artists, and you got real musical magic. I knew this would be a major undertaking since the name Motown belonged to Universal, and Jobete, the publishing company, belonged partly to EMI music, and the other part still belonged to the chairman.

I had my work cut out for me.

Motown 45 was worth the effort, so I got busy pulling things together. I went through months of meetings with Universal about acquiring the rights to the use of the name "Motown." Fortunately, I had signed my son Mario (who changed his name to Novel) to a huge deal with Rawkus Records, which was taken over by Universal.

A short side-note about Novel and Rawkus Records - When my son Novel turned sixteen, he came to me saying that he wanted to be a singer/songwriter. I was completely surprised. I'd never seen him write or heard him sing anything. I didn't even know if he could whistle. You see what I'm saying? He wanted to go to Connecticut and work with some young writer/producer friends of his. They had some equipment and they could work things out, so I sent him to Connecticut.

After six months, he called me and said, "Dad, I can't learn anything else here." So I sent him to Atlanta, to work with some very creative people I knew, only this time I added real studio work to the picture, things like recording, producing, mixing, the works. He was there for about a year, working and learning all he could. Out of nowhere, I get a call from Atlanta. It was 2 a.m. The owners of the studio were raving and screaming about how great this kid Novel was. (They didn't know he was my son. They assumed he was just an artist I was developing.)

"This kid is writing and producing great product, and he's recording it all himself. He's singing the leads and all the background vocals. He stopped using our engineer, and he's recording, mixing, and mastering everything himself. The kid is good! And the songs, you gotta hear them, they're great!

"Let's make a deal with this kid. We'll sign him up and split the management and publishing with you. What do you say, Mickey?"

What do I say? I took a deep breath. I needed a moment to think. I said,

"Man, it's two o'clock in the morning, and that's too early for all this business stuff. I'll get back with you later. Put Novel on the phone. - Novel!"

"Yes sir?" (He always answers me with "Yes, sir.")

"I want you on the first plane outta there to L.A., you got that?"

"Yes, sir."

"And Novel, don't say nothing to nobody, or sign anything with anybody, you got that?"

"Yes, sir."

Needless to say, I brought him straight home.

When he played me the songs he had written and produced, I was floored! Not only was the music great, my son had four out of the five essentials that an A&R man looks for in an artist. I had his product sent to the major record companies in New York, and within three months, there was a bidding war over who was going to sign the new artist who goes by the name of Novel. He was signed to Rawkus Records for a huge deal. Right after the signing, Rawkus was taken over by Universal, who wanted me to renegotiate Novel's deal with them.

Universal owned the Motown name and catalog, both of which I wanted to use for my Motown 45 TV special. My son gave me an edge with Universal. Working on the special, I was in talks with two producers of television specials: Jeff Margolis and John Hamlin. They brought in Tisha Fein, who has the ability to place some of the hottest artists on any TV show in America. The woman has the gift of gab and the personality to go with it, along with the fact that she is hooked up in the TV world.

I picked the United Negro College Fund (UNCF) to benefit from the show's proceeds. I felt the UNCF and Motown were synonymous. Everyone agreed, and that made me feel good. Once again I would be able to give something back. That good feeling faded quickly, however, when I found out that Universal and the TV producers were having meetings without me.

Since Universal owned the Motown name, and Hamlin and Margolis had the hook up with the network, I was slowly being pushed aside. The bottom line was they thought they really didn't need me anymore. All of a sudden, I was back in the corporate world of greed and politics, only this time a couple of new things were added; envy and jealousy. My God! Does it ever stop?

This time it wasn't going to be that easy to get rid of me. I'm from Motown, remember. I'm not going away. Sorry, fellows! Wrong Black man! I called everyone who was involved with the Motown 45 show. I brought it to their attention that, without question, I would be one of the producers. They, in turn, brought it to my attention that since I didn't control the name "Motown," and since I didn't have the television contacts, they would not give me producer credit on a national network show like this. They made it clear that they needed my expertise in picking and choosing the right songs for the right artists. As the A&R man of Motown, my knowledge would be invaluable. On a sympathetic note, they said, "For your help, we'll see what we can do for you."

I, in turn, made it clear that being a television producer on the Motown 45 was important to me, and they were gonna have to give it up. We were two months into this project; we had picked out the location, the set, and the shooting date. We had some great artists committed to the show, and we were ready to pitch it to the network, where the two producers had a successful track record.

It was right about this time that I got a call from Edna, the chairman's personal assistant. The chairman wanted to know about this Motown 45 show, who was involved and whose idea it was. I explained it all to her and told her I had planned to talk with the chairman about it as soon as I knew which network would buy into it. A meeting was planned within the week, I told Edna, and I would speak with the chairman right afterwards. The meeting was with ABC Television and it went better than even the producers thought it would. The network loved the idea that Motown's A&R man, Mickey Stevenson, was working with them on the Motown 45 show.

It was on! Now get this! Even after the network folks said they loved my involvement, the two producers still refused to make me a co-producer on my own Motown 45 TV show. I called Edna, who got the chairman on the phone immediately. His opening words were "Okay! Now tell me what's going on with this Motown show."

I knew the chairman well enough to know that he wanted all the details. I explained everything to him, leaving nothing out. I even told him about the problems I was having with the two producers. I shared with him that my love for Motown is the reason I wanted to do this TV special in the first place.

The chairman was very quiet for a moment - then said, "It's a fantastic idea." After a few other compliments about the concept of the show, which he also loved, he went on to warn me about the games the producers and networks play.

He then said, "I'll do whatever I can to help you." As we said our good-byes, I had a surge of energy about the whole thing. At the very next meeting with all the people involved, Hamlin, one of the producers, told me Universal had given the go-ahead for me to represent Motown Records as its producer for the show. The papers were being drawn up for my signature even as we spoke, he said.

I knew that was a lie. And I wasn't signing anything without a confirmation letter from Universal. So during the meeting, I excused myself and made the call to the parties involved at Universal. They said they had told Hamlin that Mickey Stevenson could not represent Motown under any circumstances. He does not work for Motown, they said. I went back into the meeting, took my seat and waited for the right opportunity.

When they asked me about having Smokey Robinson on the show, I said, "I just had a talk with Ashley Culp at Universal, and he told you I was not working for Universal or Motown , and that I could not--I repeat, could not!--represent Motown Records as its producer. So you can just tear up the false documents you want me to sign."

Can you believe Hamlin never looked up from the paper he was reading, and went right on to the next question about the show, as if nothing had ever happened? Everyone else in the room reacted as if all of this were normal. I came to the realization that they were all interested in their own individual asses and they were really not concerned about anyone else. Man! Oh, man I can't begin to tell you how wonderful I felt when the Universal people called me and said the vice president of EMI had informed them that Mickey Stevenson was producing the Motown 45 television show, and that the chairman, Berry Gordy, had given his consent for Mickey

Stevenson to use the Jobete music catalog. One phone call from the chairman had put me back in power with the Motown 45 show. I had the head of the Motown family and the music in my corner. I informed the two producers that 1) I wanted a letter of agreement stating my position as producer, 2) I wanted my money, and 3) I wanted it now.

They were pissed, yes, but they gave it to me with no questions asked. I knew it wasn't over, and I knew they would come up with something vindictive, just to show that they were in control of this show, not Motown, not Universal, and above all, not Berry Gordy! I gotta tell you, everything that B.G. told me could happen, happened! The greed, the envy, and most of all, the green-eyed monster, jealousy! They all showed up, big time.

On the night of the show, the chairman came to the taping. I informed everyone that the chairman, Berry Gordy, was in the audience, and that we should acknowledge him.

The response from one of the producers was predictable. "No!" he said. "This is not a Berry Gordy show." He refused to acknowledge the founder of Motown.

"We'll see about that!" I told him as I walked away.

Smokey Robinson was the star of the show. I told Smokey that the other producers refused to acknowledge Berry.

Smokey said, "I know about it, but don't worry, I'll handle it." In the middle of Smokey's performance, he stopped the whole show, music and all. Smokey started talking to the audiences about the man whose dream started it all.

"None of this would be possible," he said, "if it were not for my brother and friend, Berry Gordy, the founder of Motown."

When B.G. stood up, the whole place went crazy. The backstage crew, the artists, the camera people, everybody in the building applauded. They must have applauded for 20 seconds or more. With each second, the applause grew louder and louder. You could feel the love and admiration everyone in the building had for the chairman, Berry Gordy, Jr., and the Motown sound. It was incredible!

One of the producers and I watched it on the backstage monitors. After that galvanizing applause, he turned to me, green-eyed monsters staring out of his eyes, and said, "It will never go on the air. We'll edit it out."

"We'll see what the network has to say about that," I said, very calmly, with a smile on my face.

Right after the show, I called the network folks and asked them what they thought about the chairman's ovation. Their answer was that it was one of the greatest moments in the show. It might be edited out, I informed them. The response was definite - No way!

The network made my co-producers keep it in, every bit of it, Smokey's speech and all.

Needless to say, the producers never spoke to me again.

You're gonna love this.

When the producers' credits came up on the screen after the show, they ran my name by so fast that if you blinked, you missed it.

It worked for me, though. I got the credit and the money, along with the papers, budgets, and contact information that I acquired without their assistance.

I also learned a few things from them.

It was all good!

BACK TO THE BEGINNING

By the way, I got kicked to the curb again. B'anca and I parted.

"I wanna be on my own, have my own place," she told me. "I've never had my own place."

This wasn't all of a sudden, mind you. It came with a few changes in her life. Let me explain. After my precious baby, Taylor Katherine Stevenson, was born, B'anca gained a lot of weight, a lot. And like millions of people, no matter how hard she tried she just couldn't lose it. This went on for a few years. It was very hard for her, but what she didn't realize was, it was even harder for me. Watching her gain all that weight was not an easy thing, and watching her change her outlook on her health and everything was even worse. You see what I'm saying?

So she made a decision to help lose the weight through a medical procedure. It took about six months but it was worth it. She looked wonderful, like she did when we first met. A strange thing began to happen. It was like she fell in love with herself for the first time. I found myself dealing with another person. B'anca was not the B'anca I married. This sexy, shapely little bird was ready to fly away. It was her turn, her new life. She wanted out of the marriage and out of the nest. B'anca wanted to be free. She packed her things and moved out! She was kind enough to leave my precious baby with me. That's what I call my daughter Taylor, precious baby. I thank God for her every day. Taylor keeps me young and makes me happy.

Like I've said before; everyone has the right to be happy, including me. I don't understand why nobody seems to understand that! Like Aretha Franklin once sang, It strikes me kinda funny that fate is so unkind, I come out on the losing end of every love affair, every time. I hope you're not looking for Mr. or Ms. Perfect for that matter, I really do. Personally, after all my wives and girlfriends, I've given up on perfect. Perfect is not in this book.

Now let's talk about my daughter Ashley.

Ashley comes as close as you can get and when she is with her baby sister Taylor; together - they give perfect a new meaning. Ashley is the president of Stevenson International and she knows how to run a tight ship.

Heck I could write a book on Ashely Stevenson. But I'm going to move on and finish writing this book for now.

Ok, let's get back to the beginning and what started my trip down Motown's musical memory lane in the first place. It was B.G.'s phone call to Smokey and me, on the golf course. That's right! He was talking about building the Motown museum in Detroit, remember? And the television interview he was having, and how he wanted all the unsung heroes of Motown there. As the A&R man of Motown, I was one of the heroes who made it all happen. The chairman needed me to be at the interview.

Yeah, that's what started it all.

MOTOWN'S FINAL FAMILY REUNION

From the moment I walked into the TV studio for the interview, I was in shock!

It was absolutely amazing. I saw all the department heads who attended our quality control meetings.

Everyone was there - Billy Jean Brown, Shelly Berger, Barney Ales, Lamont Dozier, Smokey Robinson, Robert Gordy, Diana Ross, even Suzanne de Passe was there and, of course, the chairman of the board, B.G. It was like we had never parted.

Being there with everyone was overwhelming. It brought some of us to tears right away. And as we hugged each other, the rest surrendered to tears as well. More than 48 years had passed, and still the love of family and friends was all over that studio. You could feel it in the air.

The most astonishing thing was the look on the faces of the production crew.

There must have been at least forty people in the crew - the cameramen, directors, line producers, still photographers, gaffers, make-up and wardrobe people. They were all ages, and every one of them just stood there silently in awe, as we talked about Motown. It was a sight to see. We talked from 11 a.m. to 4 p.m., almost five hours, and spoke on all phases of the Motown phenomenon. It was funny, intense, dramatic, and spiritual.

The chairman opened up the TV interview the same way he opened our quality control meetings years ago.

"All the gloves are off," he said, "so keep it real and keep it honest. If you say something that's not true, we have the right to come down on you, hard and heavy."

"Is that the way you want it, B.G.?" I said.

"That's the way I want it," he said, "so let's get it on!"

And we got it on.

Smokey opened up talking about his first meeting with B.G. and the bag of songs he brought to the meeting. He talked about how he sang each one of them, and even though he was singing his lungs out, none of the words in the song would go together. Smokey broke out laughing as he remembered the scene. He even sang some words from his first songs. They made no sense to us either. Everybody cracked up; even the crew was in hysterics.

As Smokey spoke, he was open, honest, and vulnerable. It was great! He went on to explain how Berry actually showed him how to write songs, songs that made sense.

Diana Ross was very emotional about her meeting with Smokey and Berry. Her heart went out to us as her eyes filled with tears. Others in the room choked up as well, when she talked about how much Motown meant to her life, then and now. Diana talked about how she wanted the museum to capture the spirit and the love that Motown spread over all of our lives. It wasn't just the music, she said, it was a lot more.

Diana was great and still as beautiful as ever!

Then came Shelly Berger. Shelly couldn't hold back his feeling about how he, as a white man, had not been interested at all in Motown Records, and how he got involved. He was a manager and promoter doing all right on his own. He had been in his friend Ira's office when Ira, a William Morris agent, received a phone call from someone offering him a job. Shelly said Ira turned it down but "I was sitting right there when I heard him say, 'Contact Shelly Berger; he might be interested.' " When Ira got off the phone, he said "Motown Records is looking for someone to run its west coast office and I recommended you."

Shelly knew about Motown and its success with The Supremes, The Four Tops, Marvin, Stevie, and Smokey, but he had no idea what he could do for this Black record company in Detroit. Soon after, he got a call from Ralph Seizer of Motown inviting him to come to Detroit for a meeting.

"I thought what the hell, what have I got to lose? So I went," said Shelly. "They put me up in this hot box hotel, and I had to stay there until we could meet, which was a couple of days later. I gotta tell you, they did not impress me at all. As a matter of fact, I was ready to dump the whole thing and head back to L.A. When they called me for the meeting, it was not a moment too soon."

"When I walked into Hitsville, USA, the home of the Motown sound," said Shelly, overcome with emotion, "it changed my life forever.

"I heard and felt power and energy from people working together and loving it. This feeling was going on in every room - songwriters, singers, and producers helping each other. This was unbelievable! It was all happening right in front of me.

"To see that many people with that kind of creative power, working with such love and harmony, it was unheard of. I said to myself 'Shelly, you want this job!' I didn't care what I had to do to get it. But I wanted to be a part of this company."

Not only did Shelly become a part of the Motown family, he was a very important part of its history. Shelly Berger managed The Supremes through their changes, their ups and downs. He helped make The Jackson 5 a household name as their manager as well. And when Shelly and The Temptations got together, that became and still is a bonding of brothers for life.

Shelly was even the chairman's right-hand man when Motown went into the motion picture business with Lady Sings the Blues and other successful pictures.

"For a lonely little white guy that walked into this Black company, I didn't do too bad."

Barney Ales, my man, couldn't take it any longer. As he stroked his salt and pepper beard, he turned to Shelly Berger and said, "What is this lonely little white guy bullshit? What do I look like to you, chopped liver?"

The whole place went up in laughter. Shelly laughed so hard, he almost fell off his seat. I was in tears myself. What made it even funnier was that Shelly weighed about 140 lbs. soaking wet, and Barney weighed about 250 lbs. Now that's a lot of chopped liver. Barney was never one to blow his own horn, so everybody spoke for him. It was wonderful.

The chairman began. "Barney," he said, "was the cornerstone of the Motown family from the day he walked into Motown. A relentless salesman who took pride in his work, Barney would stand out in front of the Billboard magazine office early in the morning, before it opened." B.G. said

"Barney wanted to make sure that when that office opened, his records would be the first ones to get their proper movement up the charts, before anybody else. That's relentless. That's pursuit!"

Even I talked about Barney. Once he got started on a project, I said, you couldn't stop him. If a record could be sold, marketed, or promoted, Barney was your man. He wouldn't take no for an answer. In my estimation, Barney ran the best promotion and marketing staff in the record business, bar none.

Lamont Dozier of Holland-Dozier-Holland, who had some of the biggest records in the world on The Supremes, The Four Tops, Marvin Gaye and others, said that even in Europe, he had dedicated, well-informed fans. Lamont had such a look of astonishment on his face as he related how, in England, the fans knew all of his Motown songs.

They knew when they were recorded and who sang them. They even knew songs he had forgotten he wrote. That just goes to show you that Barney not only did a great job in this country promoting and breaking records, but he set the Motown sound in countries all over the world.

Diana talked about how thankful she was that Barney helped make her the artist she is today. Shelly Berger spoke of what a joy it was to work with him, and how Barney had saved his reputation by making The Jackson 5 number one three times in a row. We all had something to say about him, but the best Barney story was told by Smokey Robinson.

Smokey said when he left The Miracles and went on hiatus for a few years, he had not been on any stage in all that time. "All of a sudden, I'm called to do my first date as a solo artist," he said. "Man, I was scared, nervous, you name it. I rehearsed my butt off. I did everything an artist needed to do to get ready, but that didn't erase the nervous and insecure feeling that had such a hold of me, you would not believe.

"The night of the show, as I walked out on that stage singing my opening song in front of that huge audience, I was pulling on everything I knew to try and hold it together. I'm doing my thing, and as I looked out at all those faces in the audience, guess whose face I saw? It was Barney Ales, with that great big smile on his face. It made me instantly relax. And from that moment on, the show went great."

Smokey looked over at Barney and said, "Thank you, my brother, I love you." Barney began wiping his eyes as if something was in them. Everyone in the room could feel what he was feeling.

"I love you, too, Smokey," Barney said. It was a moment to remember.

"Hey Barney" I said, "I've got something I've been holding on to for years. Oh yeah! And remember, all gloves are off, right B.G.?"

"That's right" Berry replied, "We can say whatever we want as long as we're honest."

"And no one can get mad, right?"

Smokey started laughing. "I don't know about that, William R., but you might as well come on out with it now."

I stood up and started preaching. "Barney! My brother, it's about your songwriting, and all those times you would find your way into the studio while we were writing songs, making hits, and you would stick your two lines in the song, and you had the unmitigated gall to call yourself a songwriter, and you wanted part of the songs. Now I didn't say nothing then, my brother, oh no! Because I knew you would promote the records a lot harder with your name on the "B" side of one of my hits. But now that it's over, my brother, I'd like to say Barney, I love you from the bottom of my heart, but your songwriting is for shit!"

The whole room went crazy with laughter; Barney laughed till he cried. It was great! The dialog went on and on. We were roasting and toasting everyone with no holds barred. The crew enjoyed it even more than we did. We would only stop for changing of the film, and even then the dialog went on.

Then the chairman said, "Now let's talk about you, Mickey Stevenson. You have been talking about everyone else, now it's your turn in the hot seat. Everybody agreed.

"Yeah! It's your turn!"

You can imagine the look on my face when he said that. All I could do was get ready for the firing squad.

Berry Gordy fired the first shot. "Mickey Stevenson is definitely one of Motown's unsung heroes," he said.

"I second that emotion," Smokey said with a smile.

"Me, too." Lamont and Barney agreed.

"Mickey found the musicians, he put together The Funk Brothers, he kept the studio going with sessions and overdubs, day and night," the chairman went on.

"But if you didn't have your song ready to record," Smokey jumped in, "he would cancel you out and put another producer in your spot."

"And if he could find one ready, he would take the studio time himself!" Lamont cracked.

Barney laughed, "Yeah! Mickey would be trying to produce the next record on one of your artists. He was hoping you weren't ready, because he was laying in the cut with his production."

The chairman continued to explained things I never had even thought about.

"The A&R man is the backbone of the record business. He's responsible for picking the right artists, the right producers, and the right songs, putting them all together, with very little room for error. And I'm proud to say we had the best in the business with Mickey. Mickey would go anywhere and everywhere, all over the country finding talented artists, singers, writers, producers, and even musicians. He found them all."

Smokey capped it all when he said, "Mickey was not only a producer, writer, and Motown Executive, he was also a mentor to a lot of the artists and producers. He is still a mentor to some of them today. That's what makes a great A&R man, and I agree with Berry - Mickey is truly one of the unsung heroes of Motown. I'm proud to say he was my brother then, and he's my brother now."

Statements like that went on and on. It was overwhelming. As the tears filled my eyes, I really wished that they would stop, but they kept going. I was so glad when the chairman broke in and started talking about the museum and what it will do for young people all over the world. The museum, he said, will help them know they can be a Smokey Robinson, a Barney Ales, a Lamont Dozier, a Diana Ross, a Mickey Stevenson, even a Berry Gordy. If you can dream it and you believe it, you can do it.

As I close, I'd like to leave you with these words —

Life holds some mystery for everyone to face, and only with the knowledge of the Lord can we overcome the unavoidable pitfalls that await each one of us. It is in that knowledge that we gain wisdom, love, and respect for each other. The love of God gives you the strength to withstand the trials of a world in which we learn that through Him, we are in it, but not of it.

That's deep, ain't it?

ABOUT THE AUTHOR

William "Mickey" Stevenson is a Playwright, Philanthropist, Songwriter, Record Producer and the First A&R Man of Berry Gordy's Motown Records. The Author currently lives in Los Angeles, California with his beautiful family surrounded by his talented sons, daughters and grandchildren.

...nes !↑

of Largest company
in each industry are doing.
(Health of the corparation)

2. S+P 500 - (500) Largest company
~~Standard+~~   in America -

3.   more debt.   / Belled out
                      (Corpate america)

4. (Buy stocks instead of product.)
   (Don't make money buying the)
         shoes

(The snow ball warren Buffet)

Chris virgin academy.com

(Stocks that you understand)

(get knowledge)

Broker account (To Buy stock)